LEADER
BY MISTAKE

Your Guide to Becoming a Leader,
One Mistake at a Time

BY: JACQUELINE M. BAKER

PUBLISHED BY: 1009EastGrand

Printed in the United States of America

First Printing, 2017

ISBN 978-0-9990754-0-1

1009EastGrand
11160 Veirs Mill Rd, Ste Llh-18,
Wheaton, MD 20902

www.leaderbymistake.com

Dedication

This book is dedicated to Portland Works, Lakisha Cugliari, and Samantha Todd, the family of women who unintentionally, but effectively taught and continue to teach me how to be a leader.

I'm forever grateful to all of you.

Table of Contents

INTRODUCTION

I was never looking for leadership, but somehow leadership always seems to find me.

From the early days of my career to now, I've been presented with many amazing opportunities and have had to figure out which to pursue and which to set aside. When I was younger and still trying to find my footing in the world, I took on opportunities that, in hindsight, I probably shouldn't have because they didn't fit well into any type of long-term plans. (Not that I knew exactly what the long-term plans were quite yet.) But I was living in the moment and exciting, to take advantage of anything that seemed interesting, exciting and somewhat of an impressive resume-builder.

Unfortunately, chasing these (seemingly random) opportunities took me away from making and sticking to any long-term goals and *My Why* (more on *Your Way* in Chapter 1). Fortunately, taking on these sometimes random opportunities did provide me with valuable leadership lessons that have aided me in my professional endeavors and entrepreneurial ventures ever since. What's more, they've supplied me with an ample number of mistakes to learn from and use as fuel for my leadership growth and journey.

Some of the opportunities I've been afforded over the years were presented before I ever considered myself a "leader." I've been continually surprised when I've been tapped to do things that I felt a leader should be called on to do. My first thoughts when presented with these sorts of opportunities were, "Wow. Why would they ask ME to do this?" and "What do they see in ME to believe that I should help in this way?"

I remember a time when I was tapped to lead the automotive training content development division for a tier one automotive supplier in service of Ford Motor Company. While I was excited about the opportunity, I wasn't mentally prepared to lead, because I didn't look at myself as a leader.

And what do you think happens when you don't see yourself as a leader? You guessed it—you don't operate like one. You don't behave like a leader, talk like a leader, or think like a leader. Yet, the opportunity to lead a division was a turning point for me. I was not initially confident in my leadership abilities, yet I succeeded in assessing and recommending competencies for automotive technicians and conducting training course pilots to ensure accuracy and appropriate course flow. The experience made me come to terms with the fact that I had leadership potential, and that people kept tapping me for leadership roles because *they* saw I had it, even if it hadn't realized it myself yet.

And so, I resolved to dive into leadership—to learn and grow and figure out what my place in it would look like.

My leadership journey since then has taken me through eight years as an entrepreneurial event planner, co-founding and co-running a company called Opal E Event Planning. Following this venture, I moved into the etiquette space and founded my current company, Scarlet Communications. While this journey has provided me with plenty of success, it has also been lined with and fortified by mistakes. And it's this journey—the journey through and out of my mistakes—that inspired me to write this book.

I started writing *Leader by Mistake* more than a year ago, but it originally looked very different from what it does now. My first thought and desire was to write a book to help people plan private events at their home as I *love* hosting social events and have significant experience with event planning. But I quickly got bored with this idea because I realized it wasn't anything new, unique, or exciting, so I questioned the true value of it and explored a different approach.

I don't remember the exact moment I decided to write a book about building and refining leadership skills through mistakes, but around July 2016, I concluded that it was something I absolutely must do. I felt a pull toward this idea like I hadn't with my event planning one. I was and very much still am passionate about helping people develop skills they can use not just at a private dinner party, but in their professional lives as well. And so, I thought of the title, *Leader by Mistake*, and immediately bought a GoDaddy domain. As an action-oriented person, this is a little technique I use to feel like I've already accomplished something, and to hold myself accountable to actually making my idea become a reality.

To no surprise, my friends, family, followers, and clients, however, expected that my first book would be an event planning guide. And so even though I thought I had written the idea off, my early book drafts were filled with event planning information, sprinkled here and there with leadership skill development. I didn't mean to write an event planning guide, but that's what I delivered, by mistake.

I suppose I fell back on event planning because it's one of the topics I know best, but it was a mistake to rely on what I was already comfortable with since I cut myself off from looking at other skills I'd developed over the years, namely leadership skills. And so, I ended up putting so much about events into my early book drafts that it completely overshadowed the bits and pieces of my leadership story that I managed to slip in.

I have worked diligently to differentiate my etiquette company from my past event planning company, because I am no longer an event planner; I am an etiquette and protocol professional. And so, if I was to keep all the event planning information in my manuscript, then it would make me what I was trying hard not to be any longer, which felt a lot like failure.

So, I started questioning myself to figure out where to go from here and try to get back to my original intent for this book. I asked myself, "When did you start looking at yourself as a leader?"

To tell you the truth, I didn't see myself as a leader until I started Scarlet Communications. Prior to Scarlet, if someone had asked me if I was a leader, I would have responded that I am just doing my job. And so, as I continued to reflect on my leadership journey—from my first job at Subway as a sandwich artist, to my current role as Founder and Principal Consultant at Scarlet Communications—all these leadership stories and memories came bubbling up to the surface, many of which you'll find in the following pages. In weaving together each thread, I realized, once again, that mistakes were the common denominator in my leadership journey, and that they were a common denominator for others as well.

As I was trying to re-envision my book, after the minor event planning focus derailment, I attended my regular accountability meet-ups with my Accountability Partners (more on these in Chapter 3) and had many conversations with both women and men about their career frustrations. I was shocked to learn that I have had many of the same struggles, failures, missteps, and mistakes that others have had. I was also surprised to learn that many of these professionals were looking for ways to grow in their careers but were now stuck. A light bulb went off—with this book, I could help them and many others like them.

So that takes us to now. This book has gone through countless revisions, feedback sessions, long nights, and early mornings. It has 10 chapters for you to explore (down from an original 18!)—from chapters on grit and accountability to patience and etiquette to innovation and positivity.

Within each chapter, you'll find a breakdown of each leadership skill, my accompanying mistake story, and the top three mistakes I've witnessed people make during their leadership journey that hold them back from truly mastering each of these essential skills.

While there were challenges along my book journey, I had a lot of fun creating this final, published version, but I didn't want it to be all about me. I want this book, this leadership guide, to be about you too—because I wrote it for you and others like you in mind. And so, that's why you see a section at the end of every chapter called "Your Reflection Space." There, you will find three different prompts and space for you to answer them to help you reflect on what you've read and what you've learned on your leadership journey thus far.

Please know, however, that this book isn't a catch-all for all leadership skills nor even a perfect published piece. But that's OK, because nothing in life is ever perfect or quite finished. We are always a work in progress, and I thank you for joining me on my journey through mistakes, and taking me along on yours. Let's identify and redefine the Leader in You!

Onward,

JMB

Chapter 1:
Get Your Grit On

> **"**If my future were determined just by my performance on a standardized test, I wouldn't be here. I guarantee you that.**"**
> *– Michelle Obama*

I am often asked, "What is the single most important quality you need to be an entrepreneur?" Without hesitation I say, grit. However, I certainly don't think this trait is exclusive to entrepreneurs; it's a trait any professional can have and cultivate, and that includes *you*. It's a trait that *you* need as a leader.

Grit is one of the shiniest new buzzwords to hit the work world. There are many wonderful books available on why it's an important trait for success. But I'm not here to write another book aimed at wowing you about the power of grit. It's amazing—we get the point. Instead, what I'm here to do is to illuminate where you may be going wrong in trying to get more grit into your life. I challenge you to #getyourgriton. Yes, grit is so cool it's hashtag-worthy.

But let me be honest with you. I wasn't born with grit—it's a skill I've had to grow and refine over the years, and it has helped shape me into the leader I am today. I truly believe having grit is essential to becoming a strong leader. It sets the steady drumbeat against which you can further develop your other leadership skills, such as risk-taking and accountability, among others you'll encounter in this book. For example, I sure as heck am not going to feel confident in taking a business risk if I don't believe I can see myself and my team through the challenges it could plunge us into. Grit comes into full swing in situations like these as it can help you push through difficult times, while also allowing you to intelligently consider if the risk will help get you to your long-term goals.

Success is not possible without grit, which can be verified by pretty much anyone who has achieved any goal, big or small. But grit doesn't necessarily mean that you must spend all day and all night on only one thing. Rather, grit means that you need to know what type of effort to put in and when to exert that effort. Put simply, grit is the commitment to power through and get stuff done.

But grit sounds a lot like dedication, doesn't it? I'll admit I've gotten them confused on several occasions, but hey, it happens.

Think of grit and dedication as identical twin sisters—they may appear alike, but they remain unique from one another in style and character. Grit is a leather-wearing, chain-swinging badass to her core. Dedication, on the other hand, is the pretty one in the red dress everyone envies but with time, her beauty fades. Grit doesn't fade. Grit keeps on being gritty—determined, tenacious, and courageous.

Dedication is always at hand to help you accomplish short-term tasks. Grit, however, is there for the long-term. It helps you power through the ups and downs that come as you work away at an especially important goal, project, or commitment.

I want to make sure you have a handle on grit because you'll need it through the good and the bad on your leadership journey. It's leadership step numero uno in my book (literally and figuratively). I want you to be able to charge ahead as the leader you've always dreamed of becoming. I know you're almost there, and I'm here to get you to the next stop in your leadership journey.

My Grit Mistake

But before we dive into how to turn your mistakes into grit-infused leadership fuel, I have a secret to tell you. I didn't pass the standardized test to get into Cass Technical High School, one of Detroit's top secondary schools and, more importantly, my dream school.

Cass Technical High School, CT, (as Detroit locals call it) or to most high school graduates, the best high school ever, has graduated the likes of signing sensation Diana Ross, jazz pianist Alice Coltrane, jazz violinist Regina Carter, model Carole Gist (the first African American woman to hold the Miss USA title), comedian Lily Tomlin, TV reporter Shaun Robinson, attorney Cora Brown (the first African American woman elected to the Michigan State Senate), and actress Simone Missick, among many other amazing individuals. While I did eventually graduate from Cass Tech, honored to have followed in the footsteps of these talented women, my dream of attending almost didn't materialize because I failed the standardized entrance exam. No amount of preparation or grit could have saved me from this failure because the truth is that I'm a lousy test taker. Whenever I'm faced with a standardized test, my palms get sweaty and I get all anxious and hot. As I hold the pencil ready to bubble in an A, B, C, or D, I totally freeze, and end up bubbling in random answers..

At 13 years old, I hadn't yet developed techniques for dealing with my test anxiety. Instead, I signed up for the Examination High School Assessment despite the outcome I knew would occur—failure. And so, I failed but I didn't let that deter me from reaching for my dream of attending Cass Tech.

After I received my abysmal test scores, I decided to phone the school to ask if there were any other ways to get in. To my great surprise and relief, there was. Cass Tech had a special admittance system for those who possessed a particular skill or talent, such as singing or playing an instrument. If you were creatively-inclined, then you could potentially land a spot at the high school. I was sold.

I auditioned with the song "Tomorrow" by Annie, and I was admitted. I was thrilled beyond words. (See, grit pays off!) With my admittance, I was automatically placed into a music-focused course of study for the duration of high school. Cass Tech operated like a college in that each student had a major or focus area ranging from business to performing arts. With my music focus, I took a lot of music classes and received the opportunity to audition for one of Cass Tech's most prestigious musical group, Harp & Vocal, which is made up of female vocalists accompanied by two or three harpists.

The group was fabulous—filled with talented, focused, and supportive women. I was a member for two wonderful years before I was faced with a decision: take a new job that paid me more than the one I was holding down, or stay with my current job and continue to sing in Harp & Vocal.

In the end, I took the higher paying job and left Harp & Vocal. While I made more money, I lost the chance to participate in many amazing opportunities. It was a mistake to leave Harp & Vocal when I did. Although I still keep in touch with some of the women from the group, I prematurely severed other relationships. I was distracted by short-term gains and the prospect of a shiny new job. I didn't take a moment to really consider where I had come from—that I didn't get into Cass Tech with my intellect alone, but with my musical skill. By taking a new job and leaving Harp & Vocal, I did not allow myself to realize my full musical potential. I quit too soon to see what I could have become. What

I really needed to do was to get my grit on, just as I had when I persevered after failing to get into Cass Tech the traditional way. But I didn't. I let a good thing go for something else that never could quite measure up. This is not something I want to see you do.

I want to see you have the nerve to say no to distractions that get in the way of longer-term goals. I want to see you celebrate where you've been, and help it get you to where you're going next. Most importantly, I want to see you push through not just the good and easy, but also the difficult, bad, and sometimes downright ugly times. So, let's learn from our mistakes together, and use our grit to finish what we started.

Mistake #1:
You Fall Prey to Distractions

It is *so* easy, isn't it? Distractions are EVERYWHERE. I can't tell you how many times I find myself scrolling through my Facebook and Instagram feeds, liking a little bit of this, and loving a little bit of that, and not doing what I had set out to do in the first place. Even beyond the world of social media, there's always the dreaded bills and home repairs, the never-ending group text conversations, ever-engrossing TV shows and movies (major *House of Cards* fan here), and the loving tug of family, friends, and furry companies.

Distractions will always be around you, no matter how hard you try to stamp them out. You can download whatever software you need to "disconnect" from the internet so you can quietly work (such as Self-Control or FocusBooster, for example), but there is no distraction-blocking app for a colleague walking into your office and asking for help on a project, or a dog nagging to be walked as you're putting the finishing touches on a proposal.

If you find yourself doing one of the following five minutes after you start a task then you really need to give yourself a timervention:

- Checking social media accounts
- Responding to and organizing email
- Randomly searching the internet
- Engaging in group chat conversations
- Texting cat photos to your friends

If you want to ensure your efforts yield maximum results, then you must assess where you're dedicating your time. You can't exercise grit if you're constantly distracted by the internet, your phone, or other non-essentials. So how can you adjust your thinking and planning so you don't get caught up in the not-important-right-now stuff? You get yourself some Grit Insurance.

Before you dive into a new task, take a few moments and set some parameters—what I like to call your Grit Insurance. Consider questions like:

- What I am looking to accomplish?
- Is this a priority task?
- If I complete this, will it make a difference in my long-term plans?
- How much time am I allocating for this task?
- If I don't complete it, what is the true cost (direct and indirect)?

In answering these questions, you'll get a sense for what you should prioritize and what you should relegate to the later pile.

What's more, you'll give yourself a purpose orientation rather than blindly starting a task and ignoring it five minutes later (thanks, Facebook).

And so, if you want to get your grit on, then commit yourself to meaningful, focused tasks that yield real results for your goals. If you do anything else, you're shortchanging yourself, your team, your aspirations, and your future.

Mistake #2:
You Don't Reflect on Your Past Successes

In addition to falling prey to distractions, you may find yourself getting stuck along the way as you attempt to progress toward your goal. This stuck feeling isn't a typical challenge. It's not one where you can keep pushing and pushing and eventually find your way to the other end of a problem with a shining solution. Instead, what you need to do is pause. And I mean *really* pause, like take-a-quiet-moment-of-mindfulness kind of pause. You need to give yourself some time to reflect because you've forgotten something important. You may know your plan backward and forward as well as your next steps, but you might be forgetting about *Your Why*—why on Earth are you doing what you're doing in the first place? Why does your task/project/ initiative/campaign/goal even matter?

If you have trouble figuring out what *Your Why* is then, (1) go back to Mistake #1 and decide if what you think is important is just another distraction, or (2) recall the feeling of completion you had with a project, task, or goal that you stuck with all the way through. By exploring this feeling of completion, you'll likely come to *Your Why*.

Your Why is an essential component to powering your grit because without it, you'll find yourself turning your gears but going nowhere fast. You won't have a legitimate reason to continue toward a goal, and your efforts will fizzle out quickly. Pop. Boom. Kablam go your dreams, squashed just as fast as they began.

Grit isn't something you get once and have forever. You must feed and exercise it, just like any skill or muscle, otherwise it will atrophy. And so be sure to revitalize your goals by refueling your grit with *Your Why*.

Mistake #3:
You Quit Too Soon

Don't be like the teenage me. Don't quit before it's your time to shine. I know—there's that very alluring OTHER OPPORTUNITY waving its hand at you. But what is that Other Opportunity really? Is it something that will get you to the next step in your goal, plan, or project? Does it enhance *Your Why*? Or is it a wonderfully disguised distraction that takes you away from *Your Why*?

The Other Opportunity could look fantastic, sound fantastic, and even taste fantastic, but if it doesn't align with *Your Why* then why pursue it? Focus on your goal at hand, and avoid catching the Other Opportunity Quitting Disease.

If there's no Other Opportunity captivating your interest and flying you away from your main goal on a magical carpet, then you may have caught one of these other equally alluring Quitting Diseases:

- You Don't Have Time Disease
- It's Too Hard Disease
- It'll Take Too Long Disease
- You Have Other Obligations Disease

These Quitting Diseases eat away at your grit. You weaken it every time you let yourself succumb to their disabling powers. Don't let them run your life—realize which Quitting Disease you might have by looking back on when you've quit in the past.

Quitting for the right reasons (i.e. when something doesn't align with *Your Why*) is perfectly acceptable. But when you quit for the wrong reasons (see Quitting Diseases above), then you're in trouble. Giving up on an idea, project, or dream will always be easier than sticking it out. But the true win, and the true test of your grit, is seeing your meaningful goals through to the end. In the all holy words of Nike, "Just do it."

Your Reflection Space

Answer these prompts in the space below to reflect on where you can get your grit on in your leadership journey:

1. List three to five ways you can keep yourself safe from distractions while you are working toward long-term goals.
2. Think about your long-term plans. Now write down what *Your Why* is—what's guiding you to reach these plans?
3. Reflect on a time when you quit too soon. Why did you quit? Did you fall prey to one of the Quitting Diseases described above? How might you avoid getting sick with these diseases in the future?

CHAPTER 2:
RISK IT WISELY

"Nobody who ever accomplished anything big or new or worth raising a celebratory fist in the air did it from their comfort zone. They risked ridicule and failure and sometimes even death.**"**

– Jen Sincero

I'll be the first to admit that taking risks scares the living daylights out of me, although risks aren't quite so terrifying to me as standardized tests. I don't get anxious and hot when I think about them. But I do get the shivers. Even though risks are hard to stomach, I still take them, and I take them often to create new opportunities for myself and my company. Exercising my risk-taking abilities allows me to model leadership for my team. It shows them that trying something new, no matter if it's a success or a failure, will always lead to learning and growth.

Without taking risks, you may never know what your real potential is as a leader and professional. However, you must be sure to take risks that align with *Your Why*, as we discussed in the previous chapter. Any risk that doesn't sync up with *Your Why* can lead you astray, and we certainly don't want that. Yet, for every Wise Risk we take (i.e. those that jive with *Your Why*), we learn to be more fearless and courageous. Each step you take into unchartered territory will create a path for new challenges and new learning experiences. These new experiences will also teach us how to be confident and bolder in our future decisions.

While risk-taking can be extremely uncomfortable, especially if you've had the same routine for most of your life, you cannot truly grow into the leader you dream of without it. Consider some of society's more recent creations, such as sleek, electric cars a la Tesla, hailing a ride through your phone thanks to Uber and Lyft, and tracking your steps and almost everything under the sun with FitBit. These innovations are the products of risks, risks that fearless, creative leaders have taken to improve our lives. We benefit from Risk Products like these every day. I want people to benefit from your Risk Products as well, whether they are as tangible as a fitness tracker or as intangible as your daringly honest conversation with your Lyft driver.

However, just saying, "Ok, I'm going to take a risk today," is much easier said than done. How exactly do you take Wise Risks that minimize loss and maximize success? The ability to minimize loss comes with time, as most of us will initially take risks and lose more than anticipated during our first few risky endeavors. Eventually, your wisely taken risks will pay off because they'll bring you closer to your long-term goals and shape you into a more confident, shrewd, and enviable leader. Take me, for example.

My Risky Mistake

There was a job I really, really wanted, but that I didn't quite qualify for. I was working at a direct mail media and marketing company in Livonia, Michigan. Although I found the job fulfilling for the moment, I had my sights set higher. I was working while pursuing my graduate degree in Instructional Technology. I desperately wanted some real-world experience in the field to enhance my education.

One day, to my delight, I discovered an opportunity to work as a contract Instructional Designer for one of the largest insurance companies in Michigan. As I scanned the job description, I realized something very quickly—I was not fully qualified for the job. My heart sank. I was maybe just scratching 50% qualified for the position, but I wanted it so badly that I pushed past this fact and applied anyway. I knew that this opportunity would open the door to many other opportunities in the field. It was a risk that would lead me toward my longer-term goal of being an Instructional Design professional, and I couldn't turn my back on it.

My risk paid off. I got an interview, and I was ecstatic. "This could really happen!" I thought. And so, I got ready for my interview, buying the classist grad-student affordable suit that I could find. I also took the extra time to mold my hard-to-tame hairstyle into something appropriately conservative for the corporate interview. In addition to visual preparation, I extensively researched the company so that I could speak eloquently about their operations during the interview.

When the big interview day rolled around, it was so hot outside, as it was July in Detroit, one of the hottest months of the year. I was sweating before I stepped into the company building. What's more, I was terribly nervous. Between my nervous sweat and the heat sweat, I was like a walking human pool. Somehow the interview went off without a hitch. A few days later, the unthinkable happened—I got the job! It was crazy. I couldn't believe it. This job was a real game changer for me as a young professional in my early 20s. I was so excited to start working in a role that would provide me with credible, real-world experience that aligned with my degree.

As I began my new role, things went well at first. But a few weeks in, things got interesting, and by interesting I mean that I no longer had any idea what I was doing. I quickly realized that the other 50% of the job I wasn't qualified for actually existed and was something I would need to handle. As I quietly navigated the ins and outs of a major organization, I knew I had made a mistake. However, my mistake was not that I took the job. I never regretted that. Rather, my mistake was that I hadn't prepared myself properly for the Wise Risk I took. I came in thinking I'd figure it all out no problem, but what I discovered was that I needed to use most of my downtime to get myself up to speed on the other 50% of my job.

What this experience taught me was that simply taking a risk is not enough. You need to consider all that comes with the risk—the good (the opportunity) as well as the challenges (lack of qualifications, in my case). I worked hard to understand the full scope of my job, and it resulted in success, but my risk could have gone wrong. To ensure I had taken a worthwhile risk, I had to step back and realize the extra work I needed to put in. If I hadn't, I would have likely quit or gotten fired for not doing my job properly. And so, it's important that you take a moment and really look your risk in the eye to see all its colors and its dark spots and figure out how things could play out.

What's more, if I hadn't pushed myself out of my little comfort bubble of grad school and good-paying-but-not-quite-related work, I would never have had the opportunity to showcase my skills and gain many new ones that I still use today as an etiquette and protocol professional. Sure, I was afraid of applying for a position I was unqualified for—*What will they think of me? Will they laugh at me?* I thought—but I quickly realized that my fear was unfounded since it was holding me back from fulfilling my potential. I took the leap, and I got what I wanted. No regrets.

Now let's dig into how you too can walk confidently into risks with no regrets, and how you can use your mistakes to learn what really constitutes a Wise Risk.

Mistake #1:
You Take Big, Blind Risks

Many of us grow up thinking that risks must be big and bold if they are worth taking. We also come to believe that risks should be taken quickly without much consideration to ensure maximum impact. This is the "just jump in and see what happens" mentality. While there are certainly big, blind risks that people take which result in success, risks like these, more often than not, get you away from *Your Why*.

What I recommend instead is taking the time to weigh your risks. Consider:

- What does success look like with this risk?
- What could failure look like with this risk?
- What are some hurdles I could encounter along the way?
- What kind of help will I need to get over these hurdles? (Like more training, education, people-power, time, etc.)
- And, most importantly, how does this risk fit into my longer-range plans and goals for myself or my organization?

These guiding questions will help you identify whether the risks you're considering are distractions (remember Mistake #1 from Chapter 1) or Wise Risks (i.e. risks that will get you closer to *Your Why*). You don't need to go boldly and blindly into risks to meet with success, but you do need to do some prep work before you take a leap. You'll thank yourself later for being prepared now.

Mistake #2:
You're Stuck in Your Comfort Zone

While you don't need to take those big, blind risks, that doesn't mean you should stay all cozied up in your comfort zone. I know, I know your comfort zone is a wonderful place to be, filled with all the coffee and croissants you'll ever want. It feels good to be wrapped up in the familiar because you know exactly what to expect from yourself and what the outcomes will be. But your comfort zone won't supply you with new opportunities to grow, and it definitely won't shape you into a leader. Instead, it gives you the same old thing wrapped up in new material so that it looks like a fancy risk, but it's really something you'd do anyway, given a little push. Now that won't do if you're intent on refining your skills to be a leader.

Risk-taking allows you to learn more about yourself and what you're capable of. It helps unlock your true potential. What's more, taking risks can help you identify and charter new tasks and projects to bring you closer to your long-term goals. And so, if you're having trouble pushing beyond your comfort zone, don't panic. It's not a race to the risk finish line. What you need to do is grow your Risk Tolerance.

Start out trying simple challenges outside of your regular routine that are a little scary but relatively easy to implement. For example, if you want to set yourself up with a writing schedule to kick out your first e-book, then consider cutting that one-hour internet browsing session you find yourself in every morning after you wake up. Sure, it feels nice to reach for your phone in bed and find out what's up, but you can do that anytime. Writing, on the other hand, is something you tell yourself you can do anytime but *never* do. What's up with that? Stop the silly procrastination and show your comfort zone who's boss—YOU. You're not going to be a leader if you can't even master your own time. So get off that phone and get to work on what you really want and need to do to fulfill *Your Why.*

But remember to be patient with yourself. Your Risk Tolerance will incrementally grow over time. A big overnight change could scare you back into your comfort zone, and we certainly don't want that. And so, using smaller Wise Risks to build up to larger and even wiser ones will allow you to trick yourself out of your comfort zone, and into a new growth zone.

Mistake #3:
You're Afraid to Fail

This is probably one of the biggest mistakes you can make when it comes to risk-taking. More often than not, we don't take a risk because we are afraid of failing. We're afraid people will point and laugh at us if we don't succeed. We're afraid that we'll lose everything we've worked so hard for. We're afraid that it will be a big waste of time in the end if we don't find victory. Etc. Etc. Etc. You can cut failure into ten million tiny little reasons for why you shouldn't do something, but it's impossible to separate failure from the act of taking risks. Even if you set yourself up to take Wise Risks, you may not necessarily succeed. There is *never* a guarantee for success.

Take my job story from earlier in the chapter, for example. I took a risk and applied for a job I was 50% unqualified for because I knew it could open many new doors for me. However, simply applying for the job did not mean I would (1) get an interview, or (2) succeed in the position. As I mentioned, I needed to take a step back and reassess my risk while I was in the thick of it. I needed to see the bigger picture and fill in the gaps myself to try my best to make it work and get what I wanted out of the position. Only after doing this was I able to see the figurative light at the end of the tunnel. I risked, I reassessed, and I succeeded.

However, even if you take a loss during your risk-taking journey, whether it's financial or personal, there is more happening under the surface than we may initially see. We tend to look at risky situations with 100% win glasses or 100% loss glasses. But no situation is ever positioned on only one end of the win-loss scale; most situations fall somewhere in-between. Instead of looking at your risks through superficial lens, consider what happened along the way of your risk-taking. Did you gain new friendships? Did you learn something new about yourself? Did you challenge yourself and met with success? Or did you challenge yourself and learn something in your failure? Embrace a new way of assessing your risky situations to see that there are little wins everywhere, even in failure.

Your Reflection Space

Answer these prompts in the space below to reflect on where you can embrace more risk-taking in your leadership:

1. List three to five Wise Risks you can take this upcoming year to bring yourself closer to long-term goals.
2. Think about your leadership comfort zone, and describe it. Now, consider what stepping outside your comfort zone would feel and look like. Describe it, and think up

a plan that would help push you out of your comfort zone and into a growth zone.

3. Consider a recent mistake, misstep, or failure you've had. What wins happened along the way to this mistake, misstep, or failure? (Remember: things are not 100% win or 100% loss.)

_____

_____

_____

_____

_____

_____

_____

_____

_____

_____

_____

_____

_____

_____

_____

_____

_____

_____

_____

_____

_____

CHAPTER 3:
BE BRAVE. BE ACCOUNTABLE.

❝Accountability separates the real leaders from the wannabes. If you want to lead, you must not only celebrate your successes, but also be brave enough to own up to your mistakes and give credit where credit is due. **❞**
– Kristina Pepelko

At some point in our lives, we have all been tempted to step away from a mess we created and let others take the fall. Maybe you spilled milk all over the floor and had a knee-jerk temptation to blame it on your dog. Or perhaps you butchered an important client's name and were tempted to blame your misstep on your assistant who didn't "prep you."

Regardless of the magnitude of your mistake, whether it's as harmless as a typo in a business letter or as detrimental as releasing confidential client information, it takes major cajones to step up and say you've messed up.

The mark of a true leader is someone who doesn't turn and walk away. A true leader stays where they are even if they're shaking with anxiety as they announce what they've done, and a true leader accepts responsibility for their actions without laying blame on others. I have always been in awe of people who exhibit such bravery. I say bravery not in a sarcastic manner or in hyperbole, but because I truly, truly believe that you *are* brave if you take full ownership of your words, thoughts, actions, and behavior. By doing so, you willingly open yourself up to both positive and negative consequences. You show that you can stand strong even in the face of such uncertain outcomes. When you are able to do all of this, you're embracing not only your brave self but also an essential leadership skill—accountability.

Accountability isn't sexy like bravery. It's not trendy, stylish, or particularly fun. It's certainly not as edgy as having grit or being a risk-taker. And there's no cool accountability hashtag that rolls off the tongue quite like #getyourgriton. But it is steadfast, honest, and dependable. It's a skill that requires a significant amount of self-awareness and bravery to fully embrace. I like to think of accountability development as a two-step process:

Step 1: Be mindful of what you're saying, thinking, and doing and realize that sometimes your words, thoughts, actions, and behavior may lead you to success and other times they may lead you to failure.

Step 2: Plunge bravely into situations, and be willing to accept the good and fess up to the bad.

If you want to feel pride in your leadership ability *and* be a leader that others admire, then you must learn to harness the power of accountability.

But before I dive into why accountability is important, we should first explore the challenges we face in achieving it. I believe we have been slowly conditioned to not be accountable. We live in a world where, if we really want to, we can sit behind a computer screen all day and call people terrible names, blaming our failures, mistakes, and unhappiness on others. What's more, we are moving so, so fast through our lives these days, running from one task to the next—from home to work to quick drinks with friends to an event to errands and then back home again for chores, family time, and perhaps more work—that it's often difficult to stop and realize how our words and actions affect our circumstances and those around us.

While our high-tech, fast-paced culture certainly has its high points, it also affects our ability to be truly accountable for the things we say and do. Given these challenges, it can be daunting to even attempt to be accountable, but we can't expect to be leaders without trusty accountability.

Accountability has a magical way of making us care more about what we're doing—it pushes us to put more energy and attention into a given task or responsibility and in turn, get more out of it. Accountability means being an owner, not a renter, of your stuff, be that equipment, a campaign, a project, an event, or an entire office. While I've rented plenty of property—snowboards, apartments, and cars throughout my life, I care much more about the things I actually own because I have a stake in their longevity as well as their destruction.

The same goes in the world of work—the more ownership I feel over a particular task, project, or goal, the more likely I am to (1) see things through (hello, grit!), (2) take on some challenges (hello, risk-taking!), and (3) accept the resulting successes and failures (full-circle accountability, right here). And so, when we own the stuff of our professional lives, rather than casually coming and going as a renter, we are more apt to be careful and considerate in our words, thoughts, actions, and behaviors, and to play a greater role in furthering our own and others' growth and development through the responsible acceptance of triumphs and disappointments. *This* is the true power of accountability.

My Accountability Mistake

Throughout my professional life, I've had my struggles with accountability. During one of my professional chapters, I served as a Development Director for a statewide organization in Michigan focused on women. It was such an enlightening and empowering opportunity. I had the pleasure of working alongside many talented and inspiring women leaders while also becoming well-versed in women's issues.

I originally started working with the organization as an event manager for their largest annual fundraising dinner. Somewhere along the way I became their full-fledged Development Director. Their first annual fundraising dinner that I managed turned out to be wildly successful in many ways, especially from a numbers standpoint. We sold out the event at a whopping 750 people and still ended up having to roll out a table in the lobby area to accommodate another ten people who unexpectedly showed up.

While the sold-out status made for a wonderful and shareable success story, there was a less successful story unfolding behind the scenes at the registration table. There were name tags, name tag ribbons, pens, and markers flying from one end of the table to the other. Even though most guests were not disturbed by the chaotic registration process, others were and shared their complaints with me after the event as I was packing up the nametags and signage.

We received complaints from about 10 different people out of 750 guests. My initial reaction to this was no big deal—we held a widely successful sold-out event that many enjoyed so why should 1.3% of our guests matter more than the bigger picture? And so, I did not go out of my way to address their complaints and continued packing up our event materials. Unfortunately, even when 1.3% of your guests complain and their complaints are left unaddressed, then that 1.3% can balloon into feeling like a smack-in-your-face 130% once your boss gets wind of the situation.

In hindsight, was packing up the nametags and signage for next year's use THAT important? Sure, it was a task I needed to complete as a responsible event manager, but it would have been much more important for me to stop my busy self and realize that I needed to be accountable to the 10 guests who had contributed their time, energy, and donations to make the event a success. I didn't take the time to acknowledge their valuable feedback or own up to the mistakes I made during the registration process. Instead, I kept chipping away at the wrong priority and let the complaints go, only to have them come back in full swing through my boss's reprimands.

I may have failed to be accountable to our 10 guests, but I ended up having to account for my poor job performance to my boss. At some point, your lack of accountability in one area can bite you in the butt in another, as mine did.

Now, let's examine some mistakes you too might be making that hinder your ability to be fully accountable.

Mistake #1:
You Choose the Wrong Priorities

Don't be like me—the professional who cleans up nametags while ignoring complaining event guests. I got my priorities all wrong. I should have stopped and remembered the tired yet true saying of "do the most challenging things first, and save the easy stuff for last." I may have gotten the wording wrong, but you get the gist.

All too often, we find ourselves swept up in a current of social media, internet browsing, making lists, re-arranging our desk, or organizing the cat's toys when we really should be focused on a different set of priorities. I'm sure your desk needs to be purged of a bunch of old files and that your pencil case should be moved to the left instead of sitting on the right end, but if you spent even half the time you dedicate to lower-rung priorities on higher-level ones, then you'd be amazed at what you can accomplish.

Do a Priority Audit to figure out how much time you are spending on tasks that lead you away from handling your higher-level priorities. Ask yourself:

- Is this current thing I'm working on really getting me to *My Why*?
- Is there too much noise in my life? If so, how can I unplug and reset when necessary to adjust my prioritization?
- What would happen if I put this task on hold?
- What would happen to my other priorities if I continued with this task?
- Does this current task have short or long-term rewards? What about short or long-term costs?

Mistake #2:
You Don't Have an Accountability Partner

It's OK to have someone on your team who challenges you, questions you, and strives to make you better. It can be your boss, a colleague, a friend, a direct report, a partner, or a family member.

Choose an Accountability Partner you can trust and maintain a good working relationship with and whose insight and opinions you respect. Just be careful that whoever you choose does not derail or distract you from your plans and goals. What's more, make sure it's someone who can see when you, yourself are the de-railer and distractor. Sometimes we are our own worst enemy (as I was in my mistake story above), and we may need someone to hold up a mirror to ourselves to see what the heck we're doing wrong (as my boss did for me).

An Accountability Partner can help you stay on track and provide valuable feedback on how you are getting on with your goals, or how you're straying from them. Surround yourself with people who will make you better, and you'll find being accountable 10x easier.

Mistake #3:
You Don't Own Up to Your Mistakes

As I mentioned at the start of this chapter, one of the bravest steps a leader can take is to own up to their mistakes when things do not go the way they envisioned. To take ownership of failures and mistakes is something a lot of us can improve on, although we would often much rather put the blame on others to avoid being held accountable. If we always believe that whatever went wrong was not our fault, then what have we learned from that experience? How do we know that we will not replicate the same situation in the future and push the blame onto others yet again?

Many leaders are very good at taking ownership when things are going right. They are ecstatic to receive their well-earned bonuses and awards, and shine in the limelight of their own (or others') successes. But what happens when things go wrong? Do all leaders equally accept accountability during challenging situations? Sadly, the answer is no, as we've all dealt with people who have tried to avoid taking responsibility for their mistakes and failures.

A confident leader will accept accountability, and will learn from their errors. When we see a leader acknowledging what went wrong, we *all* learn from it. And so, be the leader who openly holds yourself accountable for the good and the bad. By doing so, you will accomplish a whole slew of wonderful things, including:

- Earning respect from your peers, direct reports, and superiors.
- Creating a culture of continual learning and growth, which sets an excellent example for your team and allows them to develop professionally.
- Showing your team that it's OK to take risks and try new things, giving them the confidence to follow in your footsteps or create their own path.
- Assuring your team that making mistakes does not make them inferior or less valuable.

Everyone makes mistakes and everyone has failures. When you slip up or fall flat on your face, be self-aware enough to acknowledge it and be brave enough to apologize, accept responsibility, learn from what you did wrong, and move on forward.

Your Reflection Space

Answer these prompts in the space below to reflect on where you can be more accountable in leadership journey:

1. Describe a time when you focused on the wrong priority. What happened as a result?
2. Think about the people in your life—who would make the best Accountability Partner and why?
3. Describe a time when you did not own up to one of your mistakes. How did it make you feel? How did it make others feel? Why did you decide not to step up and take responsibility for your actions? Did you eventually come clean about your mistake or have you regretted your lack of ownership ever since? What did you learn from this experience?

CHAPTER 4:
READY, SET, DECIDE

"You're always one decision
away from a totally different life.**"**
– Caroline Myss

You're in charge of your department's database transition. You're in the early stages of research and you're sitting at your desk flipping through various websites on your computer screen, examining the differences between database software. How will you choose which software to recommend to your team as worthy of further exploration? Will you seek your team's input or will you base it solely off your own expertise? Will you make recommendations based on cost, user interface, capabilities, or other additional features?

Later in the day, you're hankering for something sugary so you decide to take a quick break and head down to the corner bakery. As you enter the store, the smells of rich, freshly baked pastries and sweet vanilla cupcakes waft through the air. You walk up to the display counter and three desserts immediately catch your eye—a dark chocolate éclair, a pistachio macaroon, and a slice of raspberry cheesecake. You only want one dessert, as you're in the midst of a new diet-and-exercise plan, but which do you choose? Will you consult the cashier or baker for their recommendation, or will you evaluate the options on your own?

Do you weigh each dessert based on calorie count, taste, or ingredients? Or do you consider another set of characteristics to help you decide which to order?

We make countless decisions like these every day—some professional, some personal, some serious, some silly, some large, and some small. We may encounter decisions that are easy to make, requiring only a few seconds of thought, while others are more complex, demanding a lot of information, input, and time before you reach a conclusion. Yet, figuring out how to make any type of decision can be difficult. Indecisiveness plagues the best of us, me included. We get stuck toying with all the options before us, weighing the pros and cons, yet unable to make a choice.

Indecision is vampirous cycle. It seduces us with the prospect of help and safety. If we delay a decision, we can't do anything wrong, right? And if we look at our options from all different angles ten million and one different times, then we're making progress, right? Heck no. What indecision does is plunge us into a negative, unproductive, and potentially destructive space filled with stress, anxiety, restless sleep, and even, in some cases, depression. I'm sure you know exactly what I mean because we've all been in this treacherous spot. It sucks our creative get-up-and-do-anything energy right out of us. It ain't no fun at all and it won't get you anywhere good. It most certainly won't help you become a leader. So let's put a stake in indecisiveness once and for all and walk into the light of decisiveness.

Being decisive means you can make effective, firm decisions in a timely manner. There is no room for second-guessing or self-consciousness. Instead, decisiveness makes us more confident. Once we make one decision, we are freer and more empowered to move onto the next. In this way, decisiveness is also a place of action, of forward momentum. The more you embrace decisiveness, the more progress you will make toward your goals. It's a pretty rad skill to have, but it's not easy to cultivate. You must challenge yourself to develop your decisive muscle, and the only way to learn how to make effective, firm decisions in a timely manner is the good old-fashioned way: practice.

I think of decision-making through my own re-envisioned version of a tired and true process. I call my re-vision method Ready, Set, Decide. Breaking out the classic decision-making process in this manner (1) helps me access it more quickly as it's easier to remember, and (2) allows me to determine which step in the process I need to improve upon through practice. The next time you're faced with any decision, consider breaking down the process into these three simple steps to make your practice more manageable.

Here's what my Ready, Set, Decide re-vision looks like:

Ready: This step is all about setting yourself up for decision-making success. That's not to say your end decision will ultimately result in victory, but rather that you'll get to a solid decision, which in of itself is an accomplishment. At the Ready stage, figure out exactly what decision you are trying to make. Clear out the noise, and nail down its essence. Then, prepare yourself with some information. Gather enough of what you need to make your decision, including identifying possible alternate decisions.

Set: Once you're armed with enough information and alternatives then you need to set yourself up for making an effective, firm, and timely decision. To do so, you will now need to consider the information you've collected, whether its input from your own expertise, industry best practices, trusted colleagues, friends, family, or internet research. With this information, you'll be able to focus in on a decision and weigh available alternative decisions. The beauty of these alternative decisions is not to derail you from one you may be settling on, but rather to strengthen your final choice. You can borrow parts of any decision alternate, or adapt an entire one to fit your needs.

Decide: Now we're at the final and most fulfilling part of the decision-making process, the Decide stage. At this point, you're ready to finalize your decision and you gotta own it fully—it's time to embrace accountability. You must not only make your final choice, but also stick to it, execute it, then reflect on it no matter if it's a failure or a success. It's not enough to just decide and sit around twiddling your fingers, doing nothing to make it happen. That's half-assing the process and you're short-changing yourself and anyone else involved. When you make a decision, you must go all-in. If the decision needs to be altered at some point, so be it. That's what reflection is for after all, but if you don't own your decision fully then you can't truly learn from your mistakes if things go south or accept credit if things go well.

Now, here are some ways you can practice each step individually to strengthen your overall decision-making process:

Ready Practice: Consider how your future decision could affect more than just you. Ask yourself: who will be affected, how will they be affected, and what are ways that the decision's impact can be appropriately addressed? Also, who else's input should be factored in? While a leader must own the decision-making process and the final choice, being respectful enough to gather input from others can certainly help you make an even more effective decision.

Set Practice: Even if you've gathered the information and feedback you need to make a decision, you could still struggle with concluding your decision-making process. What you may need is a change of scenery to tap into your innovativeness and creativity. Get out of your office, your home, or whatever your current environment is, and take a walk, run an errand, or grab a coffee. A change in your physical setting might be what you need to spark new ideas to help you come to a final decision.

Decide Practice: Often, we get stuck someplace between Set and Decide. Getting stuck can quickly turn into indecision, causing us to lose time, energy, and momentum. To work on getting unstuck, consider setting a timer, giving yourself two to five minutes to decide. If you have all the information you need to make a decision (since you've already gone through the Ready and Set stages) then taking a few minutes to review and decide should be more than enough time to land on a final choice. It might feel painful at first to give yourself such a limited amount of time to make a decision, but with practice it will get easier and you may even find you eventually need just a minute or less to finalize your choice.

As you move through the stages of Ready, Set, Decide or another decision-making process of your choice, remember that decisiveness is not a matter of making the best, most perfect decision possible, but rather making the most appropriate decision based on what information you have at a point in time. It's about taking the lead, taking ownership, and taking action so that you can move forward with your plans and goals.

However, like with any leadership skill, you'll probably make any number of mistakes as you refine your decisiveness. I certainly did, especially early on in my career.

My Decisive Mistake

My entrepreneurial journey began when I was only 22 years old. I co-founded a wedding and event planning company called Opal E Event Planning with my business partner, Zemen. I served as Director of Operations while Zemen served as Creative Director. I can remember the day when Zemen and I decided to start the company like it was yesterday. We may have been young, but we were excited, ambitious and hard-working. The idea for our business venture sprung up after a rough day at work. We sat venting over two cups of Starbucks coffee when we looked at each other and asked, "Hey, why don't we just start our own company?"

Our conversation could have gone nowhere, just a wild idea we had that we'd look back on and laugh about one day. But somehow the idea stuck with us and within a week we went down to the Wayne County Building and registered our company. We didn't know much about running a business, but we would soon learn through much trial and error over the next eight years as the Opal E team. Our earliest clients taught us a lot as we figured out how to navigate the ins and outs of being business partners and managing a company. We had many wonderful clients over the years, but one of our most memorable experiences was with our very first client.

At the time, we called a Starbucks that used to be located on Jefferson Ave., right across from beautiful Belle Isle in downtown Detroit, our "satellite office." We set up shop as if it was your run-of-the-mill co-working space. But, of course, we always tried to be consummate professionals and purchased plenty of coffee and products to earn our keep. In preparation for our first client, we put together a fancy PowerPoint presentation to show them what we could accomplish. The couple was impressed and immediately booked us for their wedding. However, it wasn't until later, when we were deep in our event planning process, that we realized our mistake. We were so ecstatic to conduct our first pitch meeting and then land our first client that we agreed to do an enormous amount of work for very little money. While we didn't yet have years of experience, the price we charged was still too low even for event planning beginners like us.

For many years after our first client meeting, I kept the floppy disk (remember those?) that we saved our PowerPoint presentation on as a reminder of where we started and as a reminder to not sell ourselves short ever again. I don't completely regret our decision to take on our first client at such a discounted rate since we needed to get our feet wet and start making a name for ourselves. But I do regret not taking time to consider what it meant to accept work worth thousands for only hundreds. We could have easily placed ourselves at a financial disadvantage, with future clients expecting us to do the same level of work for the same low price. We could have also put our own working relationship in jeopardy as the stress of the event, coupled with a low pay-out, could have bred animosity. Thankfully, neither of these situations occurred but they certainly could have been our reality and destroyed our business before it got off the ground.

What this early client experience taught me is to take the time to consider alternative decisions, which is why I stress it in the Ready and Set stages of my decision-making method above and why I call it out below as Mistake #1. We missed out on this opportunity, but I hope you can learn from our error and make alternate decisions part of your regular decision-making process. I also hope you'll be conscious of two other common mistakes that occur with decision-making, both of which I highlight below. I see my friends and colleagues commit these last two mistakes frequently, and it pains me. Will you please put me out of my misery and promise to learn from your mistakes?

Mistake #1:
You Don't Consider Alternatives

As you saw in my story, Zemen and I did not consider alternative decisions at any point in our early business planning. We jumped in and hoped we'd come out swimming like champions. Sure this happened eventually, but initially we had to bust our butts for close to nothing in financial return. This, or worse, is what can happen if you don't consider alternative decisions.

Things may have turned out OK for us, as we lived through the stress and long hours and secured work with future clients whom we were able to charge a more representative fee, but what if we had decided not to take on our first client? What if we had instead used all that time planning their wedding for securing a client that would have brought us similar on-the-job learning but at a higher price point? Or what if we agreed to do the level of work that equated with what they could afford? These are two very reasonable alternative decisions we could have thought through and discussed. We didn't, and so we ended up in a less than ideal situation.

For your next decision, even if it appears simple and straightforward (as ours likely did in the midst of excitement), take a moment to step back to ensure you're making the best possible decision for you, your team, or your company. Challenge yourself with some questions to see if your prospective decision aligns with *Your Why*:

- What is the purpose of this decision after all?
- What does success look like?

- What does failure look like?
- If I made this decision in 1 week, 1 month, 6 months, or even in a year, would I still feel confident about it? Why or why not?
- What are some other ways to approach this problem or situation?
- What might (insert name of colleague, client, business associate, friend, etc. here) think of this decision? How might they handle the problem or situation differently?

Don't limit yourself to a one-stop decision. Expand your boundaries to see a fuller picture of what your future could look like. As this chapter's lead quote by Caroline Myss states, "You're always one decision away from a totally different life."

Mistake #2:
You Obsess Over What's the "Right Decision"

As an action-oriented person, I don't often dwell on a decision. I like to make them quick, like ripping off a Band Aid, and then continue onto the next task. This is probably why I need to consciously stop myself to consider alternative decisions so that I'm not rushing toward a conclusion for the sake of doing something quickly. It's a pitfall that I've had to come to terms with as part of my go-getter nature. However, a benefit I thoroughly enjoy as a go-getter is not feeling the need to obsess over whether I am making a "right decision."

I try my best to make a decision in a timely manner that's grounded in information and input and then move on, letting the situation unfold naturally in either triumph or catastrophe and learning from it later. But I know many, many people who labor over a decision in their minds because they're worried it might not be the "right one." This is simply another form of indecision, manifesting itself as a savior of morality and correctness—don't fall for indecision's crafty tricks.

What does "right decision" mean anyway? Right to whom? You? Your team? Your friends? Family? Company? "Right" is subjective, and its meaning shifts over time, even over the course of a few hours. By hanging yourself up on the rightness Hook, you're limiting your chance to experiment, learn, and grow. Don't tie yourself up too soon. The world needs a leader like you.

One of my all-time favorite quotes from the wise Deepak Chopra gets at the heart of this "Rightness" matter:

. . . .

"If you obsess over whether you are making the right decision, you are basically assuming that the universe will reward you for one thing and punish you for another. The universe has no fixed agenda. Once you make any decision, it works around that decision. There is no right or wrong, only a series of possibilities that shift with each thought, feeling, and action that you experience. If this sounds too mystical, refer again to the body. Every significant vital sign—body temperature, heart rate, oxygen consumption, hormone level, brain activity, and so on—alters the moment you decide to do anything . . . decisions are signals telling your body, mind, and environment to move in a certain direction."

. . . .

Ah. Isn't that freeing? Next time you find yourself agonizing over whether your decision is right or not, consider the quote above. Also know that all the time you spend on the Rightness Hook is time you're not spending taking action. Do you really want to be a has-been leader who was so preoccupied with making "the right decision" that you became irrelevant? Probably not. So stop obsessing and start moving forward—you'll get where you want to go if you stick it out long enough.

Mistake #3:
You Rely Too Heavily on Others' Opinions

Have you ever encountered a person whose response to almost every question is, "Well, what do you think?" I have and I want to shake them and yell, "THINK FOR YOURSELF." It's another mistake I see many routinely make with decisions. They take the Set stage a bit too far, tilting their decision-making toward another's ideal outcome rather than what's best for themselves and their situation. In doing so, you allow someone else to be in charge of you and your future. You rob yourself of a leadership opportunity and hand it over to another on a silver platter, giving them the satisfaction of ownership which should be yours and yours alone.

We all seek input from others when we're faced with certain decisions, but even with the very best feedback from the smartest of people, it's still your responsibility as a leader to make and execute the final decision, not someone else's. Don't give your power away so easily.

Your Reflection Space

Answer these prompts in the space below to reflect on how you can improve your decisiveness:

1. Think about a time when you were indecisive. What held you back from making a decision? If you were faced with the same situation today, how would you handle it?
2. Consider a decision you're mulling over now or will have to make in the future. Who can you consult about the decision? What possible alternative decisions can you think of? Write down three to five ideas for each question.
3. Practice making a relatively simple decision using a timer. For example, as you try to figure out your work outfit for the day, set a timer for two to five minutes (or less, if you want a challenge), and force yourself to come to a conclusion within the allotted timeframe. Write about your experience with this method—was it difficult? Easy? Why? Could you try it for a more complex decision?

CHAPTER 5:
KEEP IT REAL WITH PATIENCE

" Hard work and determination
are critical, but without patience
you will miss the opportunity to
learn from your experiences. **"**
– Derrick Register

How long does it take you to refresh a webpage once you've typed in a URL and hit enter? How do you react when you see brake lights ahead of you on the road? When you arrive at the Secretary of State to renew your license, how do you feel when you pull a ticket and it's number 99 and they're currently helping customer 22?

We inhabit a world where almost everything we need is at our fingertips. We can click a button and there's a box of chocolate. We can click another button and we have a new supply of laundry detergent. We can hit "send" and instantly blast out a memo to 100 people in our department. We can get a question answered by our boss even when they're nowhere near us through a simple text message. It's astonishing, really, that this the world we now live in, where everything is instant. There's beauty in this insta-world, but it also comes at a cost—our patience level is half of what it used to be. And so, while the situations I threw out in the first paragraph are common enough, they're likely to cause some fidgeting, anxiety, and frustration for many of us today. The problem with this sort of reaction is that it can pour over into our professional dealings.

Talking over someone in a meeting to get your point across quickly because you can't bear to hold your tongue until they're done can cause unwanted tension between you and your colleague. Sending out a new campaign email to your customers or donors before it has been proofread because you want to get to the next item on your to-do list can paint your organization as careless and result in an uncomfortable confrontation with your boss. Firing someone quickly after they've done only one thing wrong could turn into an HR disaster in addition to spreading paralyzing fear over the rest of your team who now feel they must tip-toe around you to not get fired themselves. The possibilities are endless with how impatience can hurt both you and your endeavors.

Patience, on the other hand, keeps things real. It keeps us grounded and focused. At first glance, however, patience may seem like a dainty little skill, reserved for the weakest among us who don't have what it takes to be true leaders. This is largely because patience has been associated with women, who have long been considered submissive, delicate creatures unfit for powerful, influential roles. (Society's been dead wrong about that.) As a result, patience is routinely crowded out of the leadership arena by sleeker, catchier, and "manlier" skills like grit, risk-taking, and innovation. While I have a chapter dedicated to each of these skills, this book wouldn't be complete without a homage to the virtue of patience—a virtue that knows no superficial gendered bounds.

Patience is a force to be reckoned with, and it's available to *you* to assist in reaching your leadership potential. Let's take a look at how it can help you along your leadership journey:

Patience & Your Decision-Making Process: Leaders who have embraced the skill of patience tend to make sound decisions. They take the time to understand a situation instead of rushing in and rushing out with little care for how their decision impacts others. Because of this, patience can also help leaders take Wise Risks that yield positive results for themselves, their team, or their organization. What's more, patient leaders can minimize the use of emotions in decision-making because they often evaluate situations based on fact rather than a gut feeling. Patience can help you hit decisions out of the park—all you need to do is give yourself some time and mental space to channel it.

Patience & Your Long-Term Goals: In addition to decision-making, patience can work wonders for long-term plans and goals. Without patience, it's difficult to accomplish anything long-term. If you're working toward a hefty personal or professional goal, it will take time to accomplish, plenty of trial and error, and perhaps even a few tears. You'll certainly need grit to propel you forward during these trying times, but you'll also need your handy companion, patience. Patience helps you remain steady, strong, and calm as you tackle your long-term goals. It won't necessarily push you to the next step like grit will, but it does keep you balanced as challenges attempt to knock you off course. Together, patience and grit make quite a team—keep them by your side as you dive into the abyss of long-term planning so that you'll climb out the other end with success.

Patience & Your Relationships with Others: Patient leaders are able to remain calm amid chaos and bring order to messy surroundings. Handling situations in this manner can earn you some major relationship bucks. You increase your credibility with others as they will see you as someone they can count on when things get tough. Beyond calmness, patient leaders are better listeners. They give others time to express themselves instead of steamrolling over a conversation. They also pick up little details many of us would brush past or easily forget. Practice patience to strengthen your relationships. You'll be in awe of the amazing people you'll have the pleasure of getting to know and how much respect you'll garner in the process.

Patience & Your Self-Relationship: We are SO hard on ourselves sometimes. Our inner monologue can be a like a *50 Shades of Grey* novel—sweet and saucy one moment and hard and cold the next. Interestingly, patience can save us from this incessant internal tug-and-pull. It's not a cure-all, to be sure, but if you can apply patience to yourself (a major challenge for many of us) then you'll open yourself up to self-confidence and self-compassion. Give yourself a break already. Tend to your self-relationship as you would with other relationships. Give yourself some time and understanding, and you'll find you're headed in a good direction after all.

So, do you think you can handle patience? Think you can harness its magical combination of endurance, kindness, calmness, discernment, productivity, and tolerance? It's a pretty rock star skill, a real powerhouse, and most certainly not for the faint of heart. But I believe in you. I believe you can not only handle it, but also excel with it—through practice, of course.

But before I jump into how you can use your mistakes to power your patience skill development, I must be honest with you. Even though I know and have accessed many of patience's wonderful benefits, it's a skill I need to constantly check myself on because, by nature, I am not a very patient person. At social events, for example, I like to come right when the action kicks off rather than arriving early to chill and witness the set-up still unfolding. I'm fairly certain this tendency of mine stems from my wedding planning days, where one of my pet peeves was seeing suppliers setting up close to show time. I have a difficult time letting something be that's incomplete. I want to see things done, not in progress. For better or for worse, this desire has stuck with me and has poured over into other aspects of my life. Let me give you one example…

My Patience Mistake

I have an older cousin named Derrick whom I consider more of an older brother. We operate just like we're sibling BFFs, giving each other a hard time while showing unconditional love. It's how we were raised, and I wouldn't have it any other way as Derrick is one of my favorite people ever. Derrick often hosts family gatherings, and they're always fabulous, filled with great food and conversation. While I adore these gatherings immensely, there is one thing that bugs the heck out of me: they tend to run late. I usually give him a good ole sisterly hard time about his delays, but at one point there was a series of gatherings that ran mega late. We ended up dining a few hours after the scheduled time, and all I remember was being hungry and irritable. My impatience sky-rocked to an all-time high. I couldn't take it anymore, and so I decided to start adjusting my arrival to later in the evening, around the time he would serve the main meal.

I made this decision to suit my own needs and did not realize how my impatience impacted Derrick and our other family members. At one point, I called Derrick before a family gathering and asked when the food would be ready. I could sense the apprehension in his voice as he asked me why I wanted to know. I answered honestly, saying that we would be sitting around waiting for the food to be done and that I would prefer coming when it's time to eat seeing that I'm a busy entrepreneur and time is always of the essence. I thought I had provided a reasonable answer and that he would understand, but his answer took me by surprise. He said, "Why can't you come over early to spend some time with your family?"

I was hurt. I hadn't realized that his meal delays were a way of extending quality family time—something that was becoming increasingly difficult to arrange with everyone's hectic lives. I was paying more attention to my own schedule than the precious life moments unfolding around me. I was being selfish and inconsiderate. The pre-meal time was an opportunity to spend more time with the people who loved me and kept me balanced, and I was throwing it away simply because I didn't take the time to be patient and observe what was happening around me.

After that conversation with Derrick, I readjusted my schedule to accommodate pre-meal family time. While I still do not enjoy waiting around, I do recognize that my impatience can strain my relationships and cause me to miss out on some great times. I now force myself to be patient, even if every fiber in my body is itching to go out the door, because, at the end of the day, being around the people you love is worthy of arriving a bit early and staying a bit late.

Mistake #1:
You Don't Observe What's Happening Around You

I clearly failed at observing what was happening around me at Derrick's family gatherings. It still pains me to know that I was so obtuse, so wrapped up in my own head. Thankfully, it was relatively easy to rectify my mistake, but in another context it might not have been.

Part of being patient is taking the time to slow down and see things you miss when you're speeding along. I doubt most of us are fully present in the moment these days, with something always nagging us for attention. But if we don't slow our pace, we may miss valuable opportunities to connect with others, as I did. We may also miss opportunities to expand our business, discover new solutions to a recurring problem, or learn from our mistakes. My conversation with Derrick was the wake-up call I needed to realize I was (1) making a mistake, and (2) that I could fix my mistake and learn from it. Derrick was my savior in this case, but patience can be yours, if you let it.

Mistake #2:
You Stick to Your Schedule Like It's God's Gift

If you consider yourself busy, you're likely sticking to some sort of schedule. A schedule can be a beautiful thing. It tells you when and how long you need to commit to something, and when you have a few free moments in your day (if those even exist anymore!). But a schedule can also constrain you, blinding you to amazing opportunities and moments popping up around you every day.

As you saw in my story, I was so intent on sticking to my schedule that I committed Mistake #1, not observing what was happening around me. If the only room we give ourselves to grow is within the confines of our schedules, then we automatically limit our leadership potential. Often, we will need to rely on our leadership skills most during unscheduled moments. And so, being patient enough to manage these unscheduled times, instead of ignoring them in favor of the next thing on our calendar, will give us access to growth opportunities we wouldn't have otherwise.

Mistake #3:
You Place Work Before Anything Else

These days it seems like all we do is work. Work, work, work, work. Our jobs put food on the table, a roof over our heads, and money in the bank. Employment is a wonderful thing, but it can certainly test our patience, especially when we're at home. After a long day at work, we can become irritable, unfriendly, and too tired to exert any additional effort. While we may be ready to pat ourselves on the back for how well we are practicing patience at work, we might be doing a crap job of it at home. Don't leave your patience at the door when you leave the office. Yes, patience takes more energy and will power than rushing through life after you clock out, but without it you'll miss the opportunity to recharge and connect with the most important people in your life: your friends and family. Work will come and go, but your loved ones will always be there for you. Give them your undivided attention.

Your Reflection Space

Answer these prompts in the space below to reflect on how you can add more patience into your leadership repertoire:

1. Think of a time when you rushed through an experience. What did you miss out on? What would you do differently if you could relive the experience?
2. What are three to five things that eat away at your patience? What are ways you can calm yourself to handle them properly?

3. Look around you and look within you. Observe three new things you didn't have a chance to before. Jot them down. Repeat this exercise daily, as you see fit.

CHAPTER 6:
RESPECT. GIVE IT. EARN IT.

> **"**Respect and trust are intertwined. Respect is built through consistency and trust. If you don't have those, you can't have respect.**"**
> – *Cassie Williams*

Every time I think of respect, I automatically want to break out singing Aretha Franklin's R-E-S-P-E-C-T. I'm an etiquette junkie and so respect is a big part of not only my professional role as an etiquette consultant, but also an important skill I advocate for in my personal life. While I'll dive into the nitty gritty of etiquette and leadership in the following chapter, I believe respect deserves a chapter all on its own.

Unfortunately, respect seems to be lacking these days. As I've mentioned in previous chapters, and as you well know, we are moving so incredibly fast through our lives and increasingly want everything to happen at the snap of our fingers or the touch of a button. Because of this culture we've created, we have the tendency to forgo even the simplest forms of respect, such as a "hello" to our colleague before we request their help or a door hold for someone coming out behind us from the coffee shop. Not everyone will understand our urgency, since they have their own lives to attend to, and so our little moments of rushing may come off ruder than intended. We have become so self-absorbed in our own hurried lives that we can't give others the respect they deserve. Shame on us!

Yet another product of our culture today is the expectation that everyone will be on our side all the time. We've become aggressive about maintaining our opinions and ideals that we may even find ourselves in a yelling match, either online or in-person, with others who challenge us. Instead of taking a moment to understand where a person is coming from and engage in a respectful, healthy conversation of differences, we take the easy route and go into all-out attack mode. Shame on us again!

I remember listening to an interview while President Obama was in office. A politician (whose name I wish I could recall) was reflecting on how the legislature's attitudes had changed toward the Commander in Chief. He noted that 10 years earlier, no one would have thought to disrespect the President in his presence. These days however, the politician continued, it was common for a member of the legislature to boo President Obama as he took the stage to speak. I couldn't believe it. I was in in utter shock after hearing this, not just because I am an etiquette professional but because I am a decent human being. Regardless of whether you are a Republican, Democrat, Green, Libertarian, Independent, or affiliated with another political party, such behavior should stop you in your tracks and make you reexamine the world we now live in. When did booing the Leader of the Free World become OK? I mean, c'mon on! Yes, we may disagree ad nauseum with our elected officials, but they are our hard-working leaders, trying to do what's best for this country, even if what they think is best might not align with your opinions. If we can't even respect our civic leaders, how will we make positive progress in this world?

While I was not in the room with President Obama when he was booed by his own colleagues, I'm going to take a guess and say that the Boo Crew would feel mighty upset if someone did the exact same thing to them. They, like most human beings, probably want to be feel respected and appreciated. Yet, why do we expect respect, but fail to give it? Respect is not a one-way street where we absorb what we need from others to pump ourselves up. If we do this, we will eventually find ourselves flat on our faces, fallen from grace. The more negativity we put out into the world, the more it will affect our own lives. It's the Law of Attraction—that like attracts like. However, if we take time to give respect, we can earn it just like a paycheck at the end of a hard day's work.

We all make mistakes, like the President's Boo Crew, and that's OK. If we find ourselves being disrespectful, it's not the end of the world. But don't continue like nothing's happened, ignoring your behavior and missing your chance to learn from your mistakes. Close the curtains on disrespect. Let respect warm your world instead. Apologize for your actions or words, fix what you need to, and promise yourself to do better next time around.

So what is respect, exactly? We often think of it as something we extend to elders, those in titled leadership positions, or dignitaries. Perhaps your parents used to remind you as a kid to say Mr. or Mrs., Sir or Ma'am, or "please" and "thank you" to those above you in age. These types of addresses are formal performances of respect. But for respect to be most effective, it must extend beyond such phrases and beyond those who are our elders or in positions of power. Respect can be shown in many ways, which is what makes it so simple to adopt in our daily lives and to add to our leadership repertoire. You can show respect by simple gestures, such as opening a door for someone, letting someone go ahead of you in a line, giving up your seat on the bus, or ensuring that everyone at a meeting has an equal opportunity to voice their opinions.

Showing respect is not a one-off thing, but a consistent act that a leader needs to practice. I define respect as the kindness and consideration you give to anyone—your friends, family, direct reports, managers, colleagues, baristas, etc. Respect is easiest, of course, when showered on those we admire. We are naturally attracted to people whose ideas light us on fire and whose kind words make us feel warm and fuzzy. Respect becomes much more difficult to tap into when we're faced with someone we disagree with or even hate (see Boo Crew story above for a quick reminder). Yet as leaders, it is our job to model good behavior. We must exercise our respect muscle during friendly interactions and as we navigate tough conversations and situations. In this way, respect is a skill you can use to strengthen relationships and bridge differences.

With relationships in mind, respect can help you:

Build rapport with your colleagues, superiors, and direct reports. Creating a strong connection between you and your co-workers allows you to unlock new communication channels that provide you access to essential information about your work performance, your organization, and new potential contacts for growing your network.

Empower others to be more productive and produce higher quality work. Everyone enjoys feeling valued and appreciated. As research shows, happier employees are better employees. A great leader will take time to ensure those around them are truly thanked for the hard work they are putting in, and for that special something they bring to the workplace. However, showing respect isn't only a matter of showering others with praise; it's also about being diplomatically honest. A great leader must offer both kinds words and timely performance feedback with tact. Providing feedback is another form of respect as it can help others learn from their own mistakes and develop them into stronger professionals, showing that you care not only about your organization's success but theirs as well.

Reduce workplace conflicts by solving problems in a more effective, inclusive manner. A respectful leader takes the time to understand all sides of an issue. A respectful leader also collaborates with others whose perspectives differ from their own. By incorporating understanding and collaboration into your problem-solving process, you will be able to uncover workable solutions where everyone benefits.

Reach a heightened level of empathy for others. Through respect, we gain insight into how others view and experience the world. In doing so, we give ourselves the opportunity to learn from others who operate differently than us, increasing tolerance, empathy, and eventually compassion for them. We also come to learn that what makes us different can bring us together, as we aren't so unlike after all.

As you can see, respect has many layers of benefits than it initially seems. Moving through our busy lives at super high speeds means we may often forget about these benefits on a day-to-day basis, however, I hope this chapter has served as a helpful reminder of what you might be missing out on. Before I move into the common mistakes associated with respect, I want to share a story with you of a time I forgot all about it and put my foot in my mouth.

My Respect Mistake

I was raised to be well-versed in the formal components of respect. I was taught to say, "thank you" when given something, "you're welcome" when someone thanks you, and to greet someone when you enter a room, even a preoccupied sales associate. However, I grew up with little knowledge or experience with the Catholic faith. As a child and into my teenage years, I attended both non-denominational and Baptist churches. As such, there are certain practices specific to Catholics that non-denominational Christians and Baptists do not follow. While we can't expect to be experts on every religion and culture, we can be respectful and sensitive to others who observe practices different from our own. I learned this by mistake.

When I was working at a direct mail media and marketing company in my early 20s, I had a very awkward exchange with my then boss. The awkwardness was completely my fault as I should have been more careful with my words. It was a Wednesday in April around lunchtime. I was on my way to eat when my boss strolled by me in the hallway. Something was different about her, but I couldn't quite put my finger on it. Then I saw it—a black smudge on her forehead.

Thinking I would be nice and let her know she had something on her face, I said, "Hey, you've got something on your forehead."

My boss turned to me and gave a smug look. "Yeah, I know," she said, then walked away.

I was baffled by the interaction. I thought the smudge was dirt, but I had clearly offended her. Only later did I learn it was Ash Wednesday, a holy day for Catholics when the start of Lent is commemorated with a mass where a priest applies ashes to churchgoers' foreheads, reciting Genesis 3:19: "For dust you are and to dust you shall return."

My boss couldn't have expected me to know it was Ash Wednesday if I, myself did not practice the Catholic faith. However, I could have approached the interaction differently. Instead of showing my ignorance, I could have turned the situation into a learning opportunity. Looking back, I wish I would have said, "Excuse me, but could you tell me more about the mark on your forehead?" This response would have created a bonding experience between us—where I could have listened and learned about her background, and I could have shared a bit about my own. But, of course, hindsight is 20/20, so it's completely possible that I wouldn't have taken the time to re-phrase my question anyway. However, this experience taught me to be more aware of what's coming out of my mouth. I certainly don't mean to promote self-censorship, but I am advocating for displaying more respect toward others and being considerate with our words and actions.

Now, let's work on you! Read on to see how you can work through your mistakes and become a more respectful *and* respected leader. #giveitearnit

Mistake #1: You're Perpetually Unavailable

I'm busy. You're busy. We're all busy. Nowadays it's almost a given that we're perpetually busy folks, but being busy isn't a good enough excuse for skimping on respect.

Think about:

- A time when you had valuable information to contribute to a situation, but you were never given the opportunity to share.
- A time where you were left out of an important meeting or conversation.
- A time when you poured your heart into finding a solution to a problem or working on a project that ended

up glossed over or thrown away without explanation in favor of someone else's.

These situations probably didn't make you feel very valuable or respected. While being on the receiving end of these sorts of interactions can be upsetting, you do a disservice to yourself and others if *you* create these situations. And it's easy to do—especially when we are so busy we don't even realize we aren't giving people time to express their opinions, to share their ideas, or explain why their input wasn't used.

Giving people time is a simple and memorable way of showing respect. Don't make yourself unavailable simply because "you're busy." I value time just as much as the next person; I always want more of it. But since we place such a premium on time, offering a bit of our busy days to others can be the ultimate gift of respect.

Mistake #2:
You Don't Listen Well

Listening is such a simple act, but hard in practice. Consider the following scenarios:

- You're chatting with a friend and they're telling a story you already know the ending to—what do you do?
- You're talking to a colleague and have a burning response you're dying to get out—what do you do?

You want to jump in an interrupt, don't you? I know, I read those scenarios and want to do it too. It's a helluva lot easier to butt in and interrupt than hear someone out. However, once you interrupt someone, your focus shifts to you and your own words alone and away from the person you're communicating with. In essence, you stop listening, even though you think you're still present in the conversation. You may think you know how someone's story will end, but you might be surprised to find the story has changed. Take the respectful route instead—listen to understand instead of listening just to respond. #giveitearnit

---

Mistake #3:
You Don't Recognize and Embrace Differences

There are countless ways to approach a situation. If you're only considering your perspective, you may not see more efficient, effective, and creative ways of accomplishing a goal or solving a problem. We may be amazing thinkers and increasingly skilled leaders, but that doesn't mean we hold all the answers. There are 195 countries, over seven billion people, and more than 6,500 languages in this world. Those figures alone are proof enough to conclude that we inhabit a planet filled with diverse perspectives. Yet we may often find ourselves thinking that the world would be a better place if it was populated by people exactly like us. Sure, that might be fun for a hot second, but we'd get bored pretty fast (why do we have friends, if we're the perfect package?). Plus, we probably wouldn't be able to solve all the world's problems on our own. Think you alone can tackle climate change? What about poverty? And how about deforestation? Didn't think so.

The solutions and ideas you seek could be inside someone else's head, not your own. Take time to consider others' opinions and feedback. We need other people to open our eyes to new ways of thinking just as much as they need us to do the same for them. So, instead of instantly shunning someone's different outlook, seek instead to understand why they might think that way. This does not mean that you must adopt their way of thinking, but seeking to understand their perspective allows us to better understand each other and work together more effectively.

So, seize the opportunity to expand your horizons and be a part of expanding someone else's. This reciprocal relationship is yet another way to show respect. #giveitearnit

Your Reflection Space

Answer these prompts in the space below to reflect on how you can be a more respectful leader:

1. Consider a time when you felt undervalued. What emotions did it bring up? How did you react? Now, consider a time you may have made someone else feel undervalued. What emotions do you think they experienced? How could you have handled the situation differently?

2. List three to five ways you can empower your team today, then go out and try 'em!

3. Think of three people whose opinions on cuisine, wine, work, politics, or religion differ from your own. How do you interact with these people? Do you avoid certain subjects, or plunge in knowing there will be some tension? How might you handle future conversations with these people differently by applying the principles discussed in this chapter?

Chapter 7:
Strive for Etiquette, Not Perfection

"As a leader, it's a major
responsibility on your shoulders
to practice the behavior you
want others to follow.**"**
– Himanshu Bhatia

Coming off the heels of patience and respect, it seems appropriate to follow-up with a discussion on etiquette, a long-lost skill in the leadership arena that happens to be one of my favorites. As a leader, you want to be remembered. You want your employees, superiors, and colleagues to look up to you and see you as a reliable resource (and as a rock star). More importantly, you want people to see you as an individual, to see what makes you special and valuable. Etiquette is a fantastic skill you can use to stand out and be remembered in the way you want—with adoration, admiration, and respect.

Etiquette aims to help, not hurt, yet I know many people run from it. Even the etiquette students I've had over the years have approached it with a certain level of distrust and discomfort. This distrust and discomfort mainly arise from a strongly held fear that perfection is necessary to succeed in etiquette. This assumption, however, is dead wrong.

Etiquette is more than tea parties with cute little sandwiches and fancy events filled with the town's who's who dressed in expensive designer attire. It's also more than knowing what fork to eat from and chewing with your mouth closed. Etiquette certainly manifests itself in these social situations, but if you want to progress in etiquette and become a stronger leader, then you must dig deeper—not for perfection, but for the essence of the situation. Etiquette can be our secret leadership weapon, but you gotta know how to use it properly first and then practice it to improve your aim and refine your skill. Strive to use etiquette well, and not for social perfection.

The definition of etiquette that I use to guide my personal and professional life is this: etiquette is the accepted code of behavior for a particular situation. Think of a time when you've watched a football game and you see a man smack another man on the rear. It seems normal because it is an acceptable display of etiquette in this particular social situation. However, walking down the street and reaching out to smack a man's or woman's rear is a different thing entirely. It's the situation that dictates what etiquette rules apply. Pretty simple, right?

We often make etiquette more difficult than it needs to be by adding our fears and anxiety into the mix. Many people also struggle with etiquette because:

- It's associated with outdated and antiquated principles and expectations.

    Etiquette might be an old-world concept, but it still has utility in the modern world. The etiquette I teach in my classes and presentations is modern etiquette— etiquette with current applications that we use to grow our careers and strengthen our relationships. Etiquette is for everyone and every situation regardless of whether you're an entrepreneur or chasing the coveted c-suite.

My approach is very much grounded in the real world. My students and I explore etiquette in all kinds of scenarios and activities, from dining settings to cigar smoking to scotch tastings.

- We may have been disappointed by someone who failed to show us the type of etiquette we had shown to them.

  Yes, unfortunately this happens all the time, and to some more than others. However, if we respond by being rude and arrogant, we get nowhere. We get a temporary high of "ha, I got you now," but the more we knock people down, the more we degrade ourselves. Practice being a good person instead.

- It doesn't serve us with the outcome we expect.

  Things can still go wrong even if you exercise etiquette. Etiquette isn't a problem-fixer; it's the balm you put on so issues and difficulties don't sting so much. Remember: etiquette is not a form of perfection. Don't try to make it serve you in a way it's not meant to.

The reason etiquette exists is to provide us with guidelines on how we should respond in specific social and professional situations. When you meet with your clients, suppliers, and colleagues, how comfortable you make them feel will set the tone for your interactions. You want to portray warmth. You also want to personalize your interactions. When you turn on your etiquette, you'll be amazed at how you'll attract the right situations and the right people.

Here are some ways you can apply etiquette in your every-day professional life:

Make an effort to remember names and pronounce them correctly. If you forget someone's name, or you completely botch the pronunciation, apologize, then ask for a correction and continue with the conversation.

Respect the setting or venue that you're in by complying with their code of conduct. If you're in a religious setting and the attire is a strict no-shorts and no-tank tops zone, then you should wear long pants and long sleeves to show respect. If you don't want to adhere to the dress code, don't visit that venue.

Tip appropriately based on the guidelines of the setting. For example, when dining in a restaurant, the tip range is typically 15-20% and is based on the quality of service. However, if a bellhop helps you with your bag at a hotel, the tip is usually $1.00 per bag. Since there are so many different guidelines for tipping, I've created a tipping guide on my website: www.jacquelinembaker.com. You can download it for free!

Brush up on cultural standards when traveling. For example, in the U.S. it is expected that you look into a person's eyes when you're speaking with them, however this isn't the case in other countries, especially in Asia. Get to know what type of culture you're visiting before you go.

Respect personal work space and belongings. You probably hate when that one not-so-favorite co-worker comes over to your desk, takes your stapler, permanent marker, or three-hole punch, and doesn't return it to the same place, or doesn't return it at all. If you feel this way, how do you think others feel when you invade their personal space? Treat others' personal space the same way you want them to treat yours.

Don't underestimate the power of simple courtesies, like "Please," "Thank You," and "Excuse Me." You may give someone a glimmer of kindness in an otherwise frustrating day.

Ultimately, etiquette is a skill that empowers you with confidence and the know-how to engage in new environments with ease. It levels the playing field, allowing people to feel comfortable and aware of conduct and protocol expectations. It also provides you with the opportunity to go from where you are to where you want to be by assessing your current conduct and bringing it up to the appropriate expectations in your new or desired situation. What's more, etiquette allows us to show respect to people we interact with and environments we find ourselves in through a shared sense of dress code, decorum, and expectations. Pretty fancy, no?

As you've learned, I teach etiquette, but I'm never in pursuit of perfection. It's a challenge in the field to separate the two—people presume that practicing proper etiquette is done when you're seeking perfection. From what you've already read about my experiences, I clearly don't qualify for perfection. However, I do have the responsibility to try my best to be a good steward and representative of my etiquette brand, Scarlet Communications.

My Etiquette Mistake

I remember a time when I was out at happy hour with some of my friends and the subject of tipping for shots came up. Everyone immediately turned to me for insight and I said, without hesitation, "I'm off work."

I thought my friends would understand my reply, since we had all gotten off from an exhausting day at our respective work places. What I got in return, however, was a bunch of disappointed faces. Would it have killed me to answer the question? Probably not. But in that moment, all I wanted to do was enjoy happy hour with my friends and put work out of my mind.

The reality, however, is that I am a steward of my brand, and a walking representation of my company. While I don't challenge myself to work during every waking hour of every day, I most definitely should have answered my friends' simple question in a non-dismissive way—because that's just good etiquette.

In this situation, I missed the opportunity to not only display proper etiquette and help others practice good etiquette, but also to embody my very own brand. Ouch. Not my finest moment, but also not my worst mistake. You live and learn, and that's exactly what I did after reflecting on the moment when I arrived home. From then on, I promised myself to remain "on duty" for any etiquette questions that come my way without diving so far in that I'd turn out treating the opportunity like another work project or training. However, I know I'll slip up from time to time and that's OK because I'm striving for etiquette, not perfection.

Now, I want to share the top three mistakes I see leaders of all kinds make over and over again with regard to etiquette. Let's learn from our mistakes together!

Mistake #1:
You Eat Bread Like It's a Meal

You're out to lunch or dinner with a client, vendor, or colleague. There's some delicious, warm focaccia on the table—you're favorite bread, no less. You and your dining partner agree to split the bread, and you dive in, munching down like it's the only thing you've eaten all day. Then, when your main meal comes, you're too full and can only eat a few bites, leaving your dining partner to eat alone the rest of the meal.

Bread is *not* a meal. It's a meal accompaniment. That's why it's not the only thing you order when you eat out. And so, when you invite someone to a meal, or are the invitee yourself, don't make the mistake of filling yourself up with bread. You want to be able to get through the *entire* meal with your dining partner, and to keep the conversation going between bites to show that you're present for them—not just present for the bread.

Mistake #2:
Your Handshake Is Weak

When we learn how to interview, we are often advised to shake our interviewer's hand firmly. Some of us practice this to varying degrees of success. However, when we're taken out of the formal environment of an interview, we seem to forget how to properly shake someone's hand.

It's a firm shake every time, in every situation, and for every person. I often find that leaders have no problem shaking a man's hand firmly, but falter when it comes to a woman's hand. Don't downgrade your handshake because you happen to shake a non-male's hand. *That's* disrespectful, and you're showing them you don't take them seriously.

A firm handshake denotes respect—remember it, practice it.

Mistake #3:
You Mess Up Non-Verbal Communication

Hey you, over there. Are you staring at me? Yeah, you. What are you staring at? Do I have something on my face? Are you checking me out? Are you judging me from afar? What do you want?

Staring, crossing your arms, shaking your head, rolling your eyes—these and other signs of non-verbal communication are easy to mess up. Sometimes we don't even realize we're doing it in the wrong context because we make them habit. Unfortunately, if you roll your eyes at people you dislike when you talk about them with your friends then you may end up doing it to them in person. Eek!

To rectify this situation, figure out what type of non-verbal communication you fall back on in social environments. You can ask your friend, a family member, or a close colleague to observe you to see what you do. It might just save you from embarrassment and uncomfortable situations later on.

Your Reflection Space

Answer these prompts in the space below to reflect on how you can display more etiquette as a leader:

1. Think of a time when someone disrespected you. How did you respond? How would you respond differently, taking etiquette into consideration?

2. What are three to five etiquette practices you'd like to learn and why? After you write them down, look them up and practice! (Or just ask Scarlet at *www. scarletcomm.com.*)

3. Think about a person you deeply admire—what about their mannerisms, attitude, and behavior would you want to exemplify yourself, and why?

CHAPTER 8:
INNOVATE OR BUST

" Don't be intimidated by what you don't know. That can be your greatest strength and ensure that you do things differently from everyone else. "
– Sara Blakely

So we've gone through grit, risk-taking, accountability, decisiveness, patience, respect, and etiquette and we are just a couple chapters away from completion! Amazing. Great work for sticking with your leadership learning journey. I'm proud of you, and I hope you can give yourself a little round of applause because self-improvement deserves recognition, and cake, and wine, of course. Here's to you! Cheers!

Now, where were we? Ah, yes, innovation. A loaded skill. I've seen people run from it like it's a gun-slinging maniac. They don't even realize that they're unhappy in their self-created comfort zones, and that venturing into the unknown of innovation would get them outta their rut. Breaks my heart. I'm here to help *you* see that innovation isn't so scary. It's invigorating! Plus, it makes you a pretty impressive badass leader if you can harness its creative, magical powers (more on the difference between creativity and innovation in Mistake #2 below).

Innovation, put simply, is the implementation of a new or improved product, service, concept, or process. A common misconception about innovation is that you *must* come up with and execute something absolutely brand new—like that bright Neanderthal way back when who controlled fire for the first time. It would be GREAT if we could all be Neanderthals again and invent useful tools for the very first time, but we live in the 21ˢᵗ century, and so much has already been created that it's difficult to dig deep and implement something totally new (i.e. no borrowed idea, no revamped vision, etc.). By all means, though, if you've got something brand new to contribute, please do—we need imaginative, creative, innovative inventors like you. However, if you're more like me—someone who's creative and innovatively-inclined but definitely not an inventor—then this chapter's for you.

And so, more often than not, innovation is the process of looking at your resources in a different way. From here on out, when you think of innovation don't think invention, instead think: change in perspective and process. When you embrace innovation, you'll need to hold an open mind so that the innovation fairies can drop some of their special INNOVA dust on your head (INNOVA, short for innovation, like EVOO is short for extra virgin olive oil…both ever so magical).

I kid. But really, you'll need to think expansively as an innovative leader. You'll need to look beyond what you're currently doing to effectively implement a creative idea and make it shine. That's the heart of innovation anyway—taking your creativity and putting it into action (and add "for the greater good" at the end of that for an extra warm and fuzzy outcome bonus).

It can feel scary to venture into innovation—I get you. It's not really something you just happen upon like a skunk crossing the street at three o'clock in the morning or a $20 bill you find nestled in the grass as you're walking your dog. It's a skill you work at just like any of the others we've looked at in this book.

It's all about practice. Practice and action. And of course, faith in yourself. (I believe in you, even if you still falter in this area).

You may not always fly high with innovation. You could implement a change that's so cool it's like driving in a Ferrari but then it could totally flop. Wrong time. Wrong place. Wrong people. Wrong color. That's why your fear kicks in even before you've even began—this point of failure. Oh, the horror! But, guess what? We have another day after this one and we can wake up and try again. Miraculous. So try out your creative idea at a different time, in a different place, with a different group of people, or in a different color. After some trial and error, your innovation may take off like wild fire and you'll be chasing to keep up.

So why am I harping on and on about innovation? Because it's a skill that's captivating organizations all over the world. Businesses, nonprofits, and governments want innovative leaders because innovation can change our organizations and world for the better. It can drive positive forward momentum and take our organizations to the next level. It's an action-orientated skill, after all, and that's it's job—pushing us to be better than we were before. We must innovate or bust. Without innovation, we can have hundreds of creative ideas that go nowhere. They sit on a piece of paper way back in our work desk or crumpled up in an old magazine we save for trips to the bathroom. No good. We need to get these creative ideas out of your forgotten spaces and into the world. Let's go!

Here are some methods you can use to push yourself to act with innovation:

Commit to having an innovation mindset. If you approach a challenge with a mindset of "I can't do it" or "It can't be done," then your new idea, product, service, or project is 100% destined for failure. Give yourself some credit—you thought of something creative, which is half the battle. If it couldn't be done, then why'd you dream up the idea, product, service, or project in the first place? And if you think you can't do it, then hire someone who can, or work with a team of talented people who can help bring your vision to life. Remember, innovate or bust. Don't let yourself be a has-been before you've even begun. "Can't" no longer exists from here on out. Strike it from your vocabulary.

Test, learn, and try it again. When a baby attempts to crawl and fails, they don't think, "Well, I guess I'm never going to try this crawling thing again." Instead, they give themselves another little push and practice repeatedly until it clicks. I challenge you to be persistent like a baby learning to crawl because good ideas and solutions take time *and* practice to work. Don't be afraid to test what you're doing. Just promise me to learn from your mistakes and try it all again (with some tweaks or revisions, of course).

Be open to other perspectives. While the process of innovation allows you to expand your mind, it can also give you tunnel vision. The way you approach a situation may not be how your friend, family member, or colleague would approach it. And so, when you put on your innovative thinking cap, be sure to keep an open mind, and consider other perspectives. Someone else might have the solution you seek to make your creative idea a reality.

Before I jump into a story of my own failed innovation, I'd like you to take the INNOVA Pledge (yes, INNOVA can be anything you'd like—fairy dust, a pledge, your dog. Let your imagination run wild). Please raise your hand and repeat after me:

> "I do solemnly swear that I will not scare myself out of innovation. I promise to honor the INNOVA in me and let it free, picking up new lessons and skills from my mistakes along the way to make me stronger."

Now that I've got you committed, let's confront some mistakes.

My Innovation Mistake

As I've mentioned before, I was an event planner before I was an etiquette professional. The very last event of my event planning career was my own wedding. I decided it would be the perfect event to close out my eight long years in the business and to kick off my next ventures.

My wedding took place in the beautiful coastal town of Playa del Carmen, Mexico. We held the ceremony at sunset. It was incredibly romantic and I was beyond excited to marry my favorite human, hang-out companion, and all around great person, Marc. While Marc and I would be in formal wedding wear, I had an idea to have our wedding guests join us barefoot and clothed in beach attire. And so, we asked them to do just that!

Although my business partner and I had managed count-less weddings outside of Michigan, my wedding was our only international destination wedding. We were certainly up for the challenge, but we didn't quite think all of our creative ideas through.

Just as we had requested, our guests joined us in their beachiest attire and with shoes in their hands rather than on their feet. Even though the sun was aggressively beaming down on us, the ceremony turned out exactly the way I envisioned it, until it was over. (There's always something, after all.)

As the ceremony concluded, my husband and I walked away with our family and wedding party to take photos. We made a brief stop to wash our feet, which had been doused in sand during the ceremony. And that's when it dawned, as my friends held my train as I washed my feet, that I had forgotten to provide a convenient place for our guests to wash theirs. I thought about all 64 guests who had joined us, and the fact that they would have to track back to their rooms to wash up and then come all the way back for our reception. While some guests may have used a water source they found on the way to their rooms, it would have been better if we provided them with a convenient wash area. They did travel down to Mexico, foot an expensive travel bill, and honor our barefoot beach attire request for us, after all.

This is a perfect example of a creative idea with a lackluster execution. Just because something is creative and different doesn't mean that its implementation can be overlooked. When a new element (even something as simple as whether or not to wear shoes) is introduced, it is even more important to ensure that its execution is well thought out since you haven't implemented it before and so you have no idea how things will unfold. You need to lay out an innovative plan to match your creative idea, and not just leave it up to chance or other people to figure out what you mean. A creative idea can play out perfectly in your head, but it can easily fall flat in real life because others can't read your mind and see the plan you've mapped out. Which takes us to Mistake #1…

Mistake #1:
You Don't Explain Your Ideas

You can chock it up to a communication error, but do you ever find yourself thinking, "Why is Donna Joeschmo doing X when I wanted them to do Y and Z instead?" Well, perhaps you didn't explain your full vision to them, *and* you didn't provide the adequate steps to help them reach Y and Z. If they happen to be your personal assistant who knows every little bitty detail about you, then MAYBE they'll figure out your creative idea and carry it to proper execution. But most people around you aren't your personal assistant (and please don't treat them that way). And so, you will likely need to spend some time outside of your creative idea-making and think through an innovative plan to explain your ideas to others and get them on the right track to making your ideas into a full circle, actionable vision.

Mistake #2:
You Confuse Creativity and Innovation (and All Other Similar Sounding Concepts)

I promised I'd dive more into this innovation mistake and so here it is: you might be struggling with innovation because you're confusing it with imagination or creativity or invention, and so you're searching for innovation in all the wrong places. Let's fix that. Let me break it down for you:

1. **Imagination is** the act of thinking of something that has not yet been realized in the present. Think of imagination as a dream, or a nightmare. It's not yet real. It's an idea in formation.

2. **Creativity is** the process of taking something in your imagination and turning it into an idea with actionable qualities. Creativity is your idea in real life, but not yet executed.

3. **Invention is** the physical creation of a product, service, concept, or process for the very first time. Invention is your imaginative, creative idea made tangible.

4. **Innovation is** not quite like the others, but you can think of it as imagination, creativity, and invention's beloved cousin. Innovation falls someplace between creativity and invention, although it may not always reach the invented stage (and that's OK). As I've said before, innovation is the implementation of a new or improved idea, product, service, concept, or process. It's the *how*. How you take your creative idea and execute it. It's your idea in motion. Watch it whirl. Watch it swirl. Watch it twirl. Watch it make magic, with the right combination of planning and people, of course.

Mistake #3:
You're a One-Hit Wonder

So, you've done one great, innovative thing. You brought an excellent, creative idea to fruition and everyone loved it. Bravo! That's *way* more than most people ever do (as most get stuck in their own imagination or spinning their creative wheels going nowhere). But now *you're* stuck. You've done the innovative thing, and now you think you can't do it again, that your innovative skill has vanished. I'm here to tell you that you're dead wrong.

Don't make yourself a one-hit wonder. Just like creativity, innovation can be replenished. And it can be refined. And it can be reworked. What's happening is that fear has gotten the best of you. You've scared yourself again. What's up with that?

To rid yourself of the fear, look back at where you came from, and what you've done to get from there to here. And look at you—you're a brilliant, amazing, and an ever-improving leader. You've done remarkable things before, and you'll do them again—just remember to tap into your inner INNOVA to keep you going (see INNOVA pledge above for a refresher).

Your Reflection Space

Answer these prompts in the space below to reflect on how you can become a more innovative leader:

1. Look back on a time when you told yourself you couldn't do something, or had someone else tell you the same. How did it feel? Did you go ahead and do it anyway? If so, how did *that* feel and what outcome did it lead to? If you didn't go ahead, then how did that make you feel? Why didn't you go forward with your idea? What really stopped you?

2. Think of a project, product, or service you're working on right now with others. How can you explain it better to them to ensure their execution meets your expectations?

3. Do a leadership-style vocabulary assignment—take imagination, creativity, invention, and innovation and define them for yourself through your own experiences.

CHAPTER 9:
ORGANIZATION IS POWER

"Organization is an art and far from
a science. Master your organizational
palette and refine what works for you.**"**
– Tiara N. Robinson

When you see a pile of messy papers on your desk, which have accumulated over the last few weeks, how does it make you feel? Does it agitate you? Or, does it make no difference at all in your mood? What about an email inbox of 100+ unread messages? Do you feel compelled to put each email in its own special, categorized folder while trashing others? Or do you keep them as is and go through them when you have time?

Depending on your organizational tendency, the two scenarios above may elicit a different reaction from you than the person next to you, and that's OK. We all have different organizational tendencies—some of us see clutter as a patch of weeds that needs tending to while others see it as a fact of life that simply needs to be worked around. Both are appropriate reactions as both are types of organization, believe it or not.

Organization isn't only the physical arrangement of stuff, as demonstrated in the examples above. It's much, much more and includes aspects such as: managing resources, managing time, scheduling, planning, detail-orientation, big picture orientation, prioritization, and mental organization. Each of us can likely find strengths in one of these organization areas. Some of us are better at organizing physical things like emails and files, while others of us are good at prioritizing tasks and may tend to leave emails and files in disarray.

Regardless of what organization style you possess, organization is an essential skill you need as a leader. Your job is to figure out what type of organization you excel at and capitalize on it for your leadership growth, while calling upon others to fill in your organization gaps. We'll get to figuring out your organization style in a moment. First, let's examine some of the glorious benefits organization offers us:

It frees up space and time. I know you value your time immensely. It's one of your most important resources, so why spend it going through physical and mental clutter to find what you're looking for? Being organized allows you to be free from clutter that keeps you from doing the things you really want and need to do to achieve both short and long-term goals. Having a system to store and easily recall information will allow you to be less stressed, more efficient, and more productive. It will also keep you moving steadily toward your goals.

It helps us track progress. Once we have our things, ideas, thoughts, and/or priorities organized, we can more effectively track progress toward our short and long-term goals. We will be able to check back in with what we've organized and update it, trash it, or change it as needed. We can recall where we started, and have a plan for where we will go next. Fancy, eh?

It builds trust with others. When you're organized, you show others that you can handle tasks, projects, and directives. You show them that they can put their faith in you, and that you're able to deliver when asked. You = dependable, and others = impressed.

It helps you feel in control. To some degree, we all like to have control in our lives. Organization allows us to feel that we've got things covered, even if a task or project may still be in process. By attaining a certain level of control through organization, you will become more confident in your ability to handle any situation that may come your way. #orgpower

So, what are some tangible ways to get your organization muscle into shape? Let's take a look:

Embrace your own organization style. As I mentioned at the start of this chapter, we all have a different way we like to organize: managing resources, managing time, scheduling, planning, detail-orientation, big picture orientation, prioritization, mental organization, and physical organization. The next time you're working, take stock of how you tend to organize yourself, others, things, tasks, and time. Observe where you prefer to expend your organization energy, and then observe where other people might pick up your organization slack. Once you've gone through this reflection exercise, find ways you can enhance and embrace your organization style and help develop and champion others'.

"Touch it once." One of my colleagues passed this lovely, helpful phrase on to me. She shared these words with me while we were planning a huge event for a statewide foundation and we had a mountain of tasks we still needed to complete. I kept finding myself shuffling one set of papers from one side of my desk to the other, re-reading and re-analyzing the exact same stuff that

I had went over the day before and the day before that. Finally, my colleague, Michele, said, "Touch it once." What she meant by these three simple words was to set time aside to complete the tasks in my shuffled pile—look at the stuff, make a decision, and move on. I found it quite freeing, and have used the technique ever since. Try it out for yourself!

Eliminate paper, if possible. Do you find that you are swimming in paper and it's hard to find what you're looking for? I have a solution—eliminate it. I'm very aware that sometimes it's necessary to have a hard copy of paperwork for auditing and compliance reasons, but the need to have most things in a hard copy format has become less and less necessary. Whenever possible, scan a document and keep an electronic copy. This will allow you to free up some of your physical space and get rid of unnecessary paper on your desk and in your file cabinets.

Limit multi-tasking. There is an interesting thing that happens to us when we multi-task—we feel good. That's why we do it. We think we are getting so much done when we try to do two, three, four, or five things at once. It feels so good because we are keeping ourselves busy. However, multi-tasking is just another form of distraction and disorganization. It may feel good for some time, but soon we find ourselves falling behind, unfocused, and maybe even a little disoriented. To combat multi-tasking mayhem, organize your time. Challenge yourself to focus on one task until you complete it. Then move onto the next. Focusing allows you to tune your mind out of multi-task noise, making you a more efficient and productive leader. Hooray!

As with other leadership skills discussed in this book, organization requires practice and patience to master. I am always improving in this leadership area myself, and had to completely re-envision my organization style when I moved out to Washington, D.C.

My Organization Mistake

As I closed out my event planning company in Detroit and prepared to become a full-time Washington, D.C. transplant, I didn't fully realize everything I was leaving behind. In Detroit, I had a fulfilling career as a wedding planner and attracted many wonderful clients. I harnessed this energy and used the momentum to launch my etiquette company, Scarlet Communications. While I still maintain Scarlet Communications clients in Detroit, lots of my work naturally shifted to the Washington, D.C. area. My work may have moved with me, but my network sure didn't. Even though I was steadily growing Scarlet Communications, I had to re-organize myself to ensure my company would grow strong even in the face of a recent move.

Since I did not yet have a strong contact network in D.C., I quickly realized that what got me here would not get me there. What I mean by this is that whatever you used to get wherever you were in your past is not necessarily the process that will get you to where you want to go in the future. And so, I had to re-think the way I networked and strategized. I had to figure out a new way to engage with people as D.C. peeps were different from my Detroit ones. I initially made some mistakes during this process because I attempted to fit the organization style I used in Detroit to my D.C. work to complete tasks and manage relationships. Eventually, I learned to refine my organization style and tailor it to wherever I found myself geographically, as my business has grown so much so that I've now taught etiquette in 13 different states, and hope to teach in many more over the next several years.

My move turned out to be one of my biggest learning journeys to date. I was no longer a big fish in a small pond. I was now a very small fish in a very large pond and I needed to figure out how to swim again. I'm happy to report that I'm swimming, and swimming strong these days. I've developed a strong social and professional network, and I've found my organization groove again. Now, I'd like to help you find yours. On to the mistakes!

Mistake #1:
You Think Everyone Should Be as Organized as You

I've said it before, and I've heard others say it too: "Why can't you be organized like me?" This question assumes that your organization style or system is somehow superior to another's. While there are ways to enhance and refine our organization styles and to customize them to a particular situation, there is no such thing as having a superior sense of organization. Rather, we all have a different organization tendency, and it can be easy to overlook another's organization strength if it doesn't sync up with your own.

You best be careful of this common pitfall, especially when dealing with your team. Don't make the mistake of undervaluing and disrespecting a colleague simply because their organization style differs from yours. Embrace what they bring to the table and allow them to fill any gaps in your own organization process.

Mistake #2:
You Focus on Perfection

Organization does not equal perfection just as etiquette does not equal perfection. Perfection is unattainable, that's why it's called perfection, not good enough. Organization, however, is highly attainable. You can learn to enhance your current organization style and create a new one or adapt an old one for new situations, people, resources, tasks, and priorities. What we get hung up on is Mistake #1, where we think our organization powers are higher than someone else's. This sets us up with a mindset that anything below our subjective organization standards are imperfect. This in a trap. It narrows your focus so much so it's only focused on you! You must expand your view if you want to be a leader, as it must encompass the organization styles of others if you want any chance of success.

Mistake #3:
You Try to Do It All

How many times have you committed to something and later regretted that decision? Would it have been easier if you would have learned to say "no" or learned how to delegate things to others around you?

Most seasoned leaders learn, usually through trial and error, that they must be able to tactfully and gracefully refuse to take on what they cannot handle. Remember, organization doesn't mean that you need to do it all. It means you need to learn how to take on what's important and how to get help from others around you.

Getting help from others can be a challenge if you're someone who thinks, "but people just don't do it like me" or "I'll just do it myself." While it's completely understandable that you want things done a certain way, hoarding tasks can cause these outcomes:

- Other people will never learn how to do the task correctly, so you could be stuck expecting to complete the task forever.
- You won't have the opportunity to do more exciting and interesting projects because you'll be consumed with doing the same old stuff.
- You'll miss the opportunity to coach and mentor a future leader.

You do not have to do it all. I repeat: YOU DO NOT HAVE TO DO IT ALL. Learning to organize, by prioritizing what's important and letting go of what you cannot do, will minimize stress, missed deadlines, and false expectations. You can achieve this primarily through delegation. Yes—delegate what you can't onto someone else who can.

Be careful, though. Delegation doesn't mean haphazardly passing off all the stuff that you don't want to do. Delegation is the act of thoughtfully considering who might benefit from being responsible for a particular task. For example, if you have to organize the team retreat, but you know that one of your colleagues has much more experience in this area and enjoys doing it, perhaps you can partner with them or delegate the responsibility entirely to them.

Embrace the power of organization through delegation and you'll get much more done than you thought you ever would thanks to the help of others.

Your Reflection Space

Answer these prompts in the space below to reflect on how you can become a more organized leader:

1. Think of one or two folders of documents you currently have in your office. Can you make them into electronic files? If so, how will you store them and where? Create a plan for yourself to start your file migration.

2. Think about two or three people you currently work with whose organization styles differ from your own. The next time you work with them, how can you acknowledge and celebrate their style? And how can you call upon their organization strengths for your new project?

3. Write down three to five tasks you can delegate to someone else, and then write down who that someone else could be. Review your list, and then ask for some help!

CHAPTER 10:
CHOOSE POSITIVITY

"I know for sure that what we dwell on is who we become."
– Oprah Winfrey

Positivity. Yawn. Am I right? We see it paraded around everywhere—magazines, newsletters, blogs, newspapers, TV, and social media—like it's a skill sent straight from the gods. Everyone keeps encouraging us to "be positive" and that it will solve our problems. I hate to burst the unrealistic positivity bubble, but it won't solve *all* of our problems. It will solve some, however.

Like etiquette, positivity has the power to shape our circumstances, making the bad seem a little less bad and the good seem close to perfection. It's a filter we can fit onto our lives to enhance the view. What's more, being positive, even when things look bleak, takes guts and true leadership. It forces you to step outside your regular thinking and processes to accept a new reality—one that's brighter, bolder, more encouraging, and more optimistic.

Nowadays, it's virtually impossible to skim a news feed on social media or walk past a TV without reading or seeing highly negative messages. The message could be from a trolling Neo-Nazi on Twitter or E! News telling you your thighs are too fat. Succumbing to these types of messages is easy to do. We are enveloped in negativity daily. While the world may be sending us messages of positivity, it's also encouraging us to be negative. It's a battle, and it's your choice to decide which side will win you over.

What will truly elevate you as a leader and as a person is your mindset, and that's why I've saved this chapter as my last in this book. If you choose a negative mindset, you automatically disadvantage yourself since everything is full of "can't," therefore you won't accomplish much of anything. However, if you choose a positive mindset, you give yourself an advantage—you can see the good even when surrounded by the bad, elevating you above the noise and into a heightened state of awareness and openness. What's more, a positive mindset places you in the good graces of many. You will be someone people actually want to be around.

Think about this: would you like to work for a cynical, negative person? Would you feel motivated if you were constantly surrounded by such individuals? How would employee morale suffer at the hands of such leadership?

We all know the answers to these questions, because many of us are working or have worked in environments where we have to deal with these negativity-induced issues. No one enjoys being surrounded by constant pessimism in any space of their life. It makes you feel rotten and downtrodden. What's more, negativity deters growth, so you better get away from it with a 10-foot pole.

But let me be honest and transparent here—being continuously positive is hard. While it ain't easy, it's not impossible! Making small adjustments to your everyday life will help you stay on a positive path. Try these simple, easy tactics on for size:

Make it a point to express gratitude to five individuals once a week either electronically or face-to-face.

Limit your interactions with people who are notoriously negative, as their attitude and behavior will eventually rub off on you.

Pause and take a deep breath when you get the urge to complain, and then think about what you have to be thankful for, and appreciate it in the moment.

Address and manage the negative self-talk. Negative self-talk impacts your ability to be great and will cause you to be negative to others as well. Accept that, as humans, we all have our faults, but the ability to forgive ourselves and take pride in who we are helps us become confident and happy.

Positivity is like a magnet. Once you've embraced the power that it can shower on your life, you will notice that others around you will follow your example and will be attracted to not just you, but also to what you have to say and offer.

Being positive is a beautiful feeling, a feeling of lightness, of happiness, of calmness. And, more importantly, choosing positivity is empowering because it's an active choice that *you* make and are responsible for and accountable to.

My Positivity Mistake

In general, I am a positive person, but I've had my struggles with it just like with every leadership skill in this book. Thinking back to my early years teaching etiquette, I remember giving an etiquette training for a college program at Second Ebenezer Church in Detroit. The day started out rocky with a late start, low tire pressure—the whole nine. When I arrived at the church, my then teaching assistant, Ashley, was already there ready to rock and roll per usual. I could always count on Ashley to keep things cool, steady, professional, and positive.

When we started setting up for the program, we discovered that the technology cords were not long enough to span from my laptop to the projector. I remember saying to Ashley, "Well, this isn't going to work. We may as well pack it up."

I can so clearly remember the look on Ashley's face all these years later. She gave me her best "like heck we are" look, and kept on working away, trying to make this program happen.

As we continued with set-up, thing after thing went wrong, and each time I responded in a defeated way. As if on cue, Ashley gave me that look of hers each time that made me check myself.

After overcoming about five more hurdles, we were set and ready to go. The class turned out exactly as we'd planned it (minus the rocky start). It was engaging, informative, and motivating, and the students were fantastic. Even with all the early set-up issues, we managed to pull off another great etiquette lesson. My negativity was completely unfounded, it turned out, as it most often is.

I can recall several times in my professional life when my initial desire, facing a challenge straight on, was to succumb to the feeling of defeat. But, I can also recall more times than these where I pushed through the obstacles with optimism and finished what I started, enjoying the sweet victory. Ashley certainly helped me in my story above, but I also needed to do some of the heavy lifting myself. I've learned that that only way to combat feelings of defeat, fear, and negativity are with a healthy dose of positivity paired with grit. So #getyourgriton and inject some positivity into your life.

Mistake #1:
You Don't Change Your Language

It's like you're stuck on repeat, playing the same negativity message over and over again. I get stuck sometimes too, as you witnessed in my story above. It's hard to rewrite the negative messages we tell ourselves and that we let out into the world. But it is possible. It just takes some practice to make our revised positive messages stick.

The next time you're tempted to pull out an "I can't," "You can't," "They can't," "That's stupid," "This won't work," "This will fail," or some other iteration of these phrases, force yourself to revise before you let the negative words slip out of your mouth. Change these can't-do phrases to can-do ones like, "I can and will, "I believe in you," I believe in them," "This isn't quite right yet, but it's getting there," and "We can make this work; it may just take some time."

Do you see how the second set of phrases feels different from the first? They're not overwhelming gushy, but they are positive and forward looking. This is the type of energy you want to strive for within yourself as well as within your team. The more you can channel these positive phrases and bat away the negative ones, the greater likelihood you and those around you will meet with success.

As I said, revising our internal and external messages takes practice in addition to significant self-restraint. And practice won't make perfect in this case, but it will make better. So I challenge you do better and be better—be positive.

Mistake #2:
You're Missing a Positivity Partner

A Positivity Partner is like an Accountability Partner, but for positivity. Pretty straightforward. They can be one of the same, or two different partners. You could also ask several of your favorite peeps to serve as Positivity Partners. In my story, Ashley served as my Positivity Partner. She checked me when I grew too negative with our situation. And that's exactly what a Positivity Partner should do—let you know when you're stuck in a negative dump and then help pull you out when you have trouble picking yourself up.

Mistake #3:
You Don't Acknowledge the Good in Each New Day

There is something good in every single day of our lives—no matter how many crappy moments may crowd themselves into our days. There is always something to be grateful for—something to look at in awe, something to wonder about, something to laugh about, something to smile about, something to dream about. Instead of going through your day as a Negative Nancy or a No-No Ned, try on a Gratitude Hat for size.

The beauty of an intangible Gratitude Hat is that you can slip it on and off throughout the day. I understand—we can't be grateful every single moment of every single day. Even gratitude must be done in moderation to avoid overexertion. But having a Gratitude Hat means it's *your* choice to put it on or take it off—yours and yours alone. That means we have control over whether or not we acknowledge the good in each new day. When we do, we increase the likelihood that we'll see more good things throughout the day. It also increases the probability that we will treat those around us with respect, patience, and consideration, as a true leader should.

Now, before I let you go into the world with a newly fashioned Gratitude Hat, I'd like to leave you with this inspiring quote from Pamela Owens Renfro:

....

"There is good in life every day. Take a few minutes to distract yourself from your concerns—long enough to draw strength from a tree or to find pleasure in a bird's song. Return a smile; realize that life is a series of levels, cycles of ups and downs—some easy, some challenging. Through it all, you will learn; you will grow strong in faith; you will mature in understanding. The difficult times are often the best teachers, and there is good to be found in all situations. Reach for the good. Be positive, and don't give up."

....

Your Reflection Space

Answer these prompts in the space below to reflect on how you can become a more positive leader:

1. What do you do if someone mispronounces your name? How do you correct them without being mean?

2. List a few negative self-talk phrases that circle in your mind from time to time. Cross them out. Now list positive self-talk phrases you can replace the negative ones with. Say them out loud to yourself. Practice them each day like affirmations. Make them habit, and learn to believe them.

3. Make a list of three to five people who could serve as your Positivity Partners. Why did you think of them? How can they help hold you accountable to positivity?

Thank You!

Thank you for joining me on the *Leader by Mistake* journey! I appreciate your support for the book and I hope you'll help continue the conversation at *www.leaderbymistake.com*.

While you're there, create your own complimentary *Leader by Mistake* profile and share it. Join in on the website conversation and join the Facebook group. Also, be sure to search for and use the hashtag #leaderbymistake on social media.

I wish you all the best on your leadership journey—and I look forward to hearing from you as you learn and grow from your mistakes and mine!

JMB

Acknowledgements

The creation and production of *Leader by Mistake* was truly a feat, one that was much more intricate than I could have ever imagined. Many thanks to those listed below, and many others who quietly cheered, encouraged, and supported from afar:

- Marc Baker – husband, favorite human, and supporter of *Leader by Mistake* initiatives (and all the other ones), whether they turn out great, good, bad, or flat out ugly
- Kristina Pepelko – *Leader by Mistake* book editor, #cashcat companion (although I'm not into cats), and all-around book and content contributor
- Cherice Williams – *Leader by Mistake* marketing consultant, strategist, and secret Accountability Partner
- Andrea Williams – *Leader by Mistake* book cover designer and super friend
- Thaddeus Johnson – *Leader by Mistake* website designer
- Tanish Stiger – Accountability Partner and project advocate

Thank you for your inspiration and your content contributions to *Leader by Mistake*: Derrick Register, Cassie Williams, Tiara N. Robinson, Zemen Marrugi, Ashley Goodwin, Lisa Bradley Mitchell, Therese Peace, Patricia Terry-Ross, Michele Lewis Watts and Carlton White.

Thank you for your consistent support and feedback on this book endeavor: Aleechia Reese, Rajoielle Register, Brandi Rolston, Maria Weathington, Kenzie Current, Jennifer Peeples,

Cassie Williams, the Ladies of 12 Days DC Metro, Tiffany Newton, Alexis Abramson, Jessica Ekong, Shewana Skinner, Quentin Love, and Lori Kitchen.

And, thank you to all book cover survey participants: Devoreaux Walton, Melinda MeMe Anderson, Yodit Mesfin Johnson, Tonya Banks, Jamila Dorsey, Andria's Bellame, Angela Pinchem, Sheila Grant, Kena Johnson, Michelle Ponton, Tafari Stevenson Howard, Sommer Woods, Vanessa Givhan, Morgan K. McDonaldson, Emily Dixon, Byron Suggs, Karla Jones, Dawn Oliver, Kazzie K. Cooper, Jernell Alexander, Christianne Sims, Brandi White, Tatiana Grant, Kelley Suggs, Frenchie Davis, Robin Dillard, Deidra Hogue, Geraine Whiteside, Aisha Taylor, and Brittni Brown.

ABOUT
THE AUTHOR

Jacqueline M. Baker is a leading consultant in the areas of etiquette and protocol. Following nearly a decade-long career dedicated to wedding and event planning, Jacqueline founded Scarlet Communications to provide etiquette and employee engagement consulting and coaching. She strategically works to create solutions and discover opportunities that will further the growth of organizations and arm youth, employees, athletes, entrepreneurs, and executives with the critical life skills that will foster positive and productive business and personal lifestyles.

Jacqueline takes a modern and innovative approach to etiquette training, design, and facilitation. While the origins of etiquette span back several centuries, Jacqueline respects those traditions while making the everyday practices relevant, efficient, and effective for today's usage.

Using the Engage, Enlighten, and Empower model of Scarlet Communications, Jacqueline has coached over 5,000 people across 13 states in business etiquette and life skills and has worked with an array of organizations including, two NFL teams, Nike, Deloitte, Ernst & Young, UAW Ford, and the Department of Defense. Jacqueline has been featured in a number of media outlets, including *Essence Magazine*, Detroit Public Television, *Tom Joyner TV*, NBC (WDIV-TV 14), and CBS (WUSA 9), for her unique approach to etiquette instruction.

Jacqueline has also served in leadership and management roles providing training, consulting, public relations, and event management to organizations including AT&T, Chrysler, and Ford Motor Company. She is presently a Senior Advisor at a DC-based non profit.

As a Certified Six-Sigma Greenbelt, Jacqueline consistently develops systems to aid clients in streamlining processes to assist in reaching their strategic planning and development goals.

Jacqueline is originally from Detroit, Michigan and currently lives in the Washington D.C. area with her husband, Marc, where they enjoy hosting dinner parties and events for their friends and family.

Made in the USA
Middletown, DE
02 July 2019